MW00814279

Silk
The Thread that
Tied the World

Silk
The Thread that Tied the World

Anthony Burton

PEN & SWORD HISTORY

AN IMPRINT OF PEN & SWORD BOOKS LTD.
YORKSHIRE - PHILADELPHIA

First published in Great Britain in 2021 by
Pen and Sword History
An imprint of
Pen & Sword Books Ltd
Yorkshire - Philadelphia

ISBN 978 1 52678 092 8

Typeset in 10.5/13.5 pt Palatino
Typeset by SJmagic DESIGN SERVICES, India.

Printed and bound in India by Replika Press Pvt. Ltd.

Pen & Sword Books Ltd incorporates the Imprints of Pen & Sword Books Archaeology, Atlas, Aviation, Battleground, Discovery, Family History, History, Maritime, Military, Naval, Politics, Railways, Select, Transport, True Crime, Fiction, Frontline Books, Leo Cooper, Praetorian Press, Seaforth Publishing, Wharncliffe and White Owl.

For a complete list of Pen & Sword titles please contact

PEN & SWORD BOOKS LIMITED
47 Church Street, Barnsley, South Yorkshire, S70 2AS, England
E-mail: enquiries@pen-and-sword.co.uk
Website: www.pen-and-sword.co.uk

or

PEN AND SWORD BOOKS
1950 Lawrence Rd, Havertown, PA 19083, USA
E-mail: Uspen-and-sword@casematepublishers.com
Website: www.penandswordbooks.com

Contents

Acknowledgements

The author wishes to thank to thank the following for providing the illustrations on the pages shown below 13, Maigorzala Milaszewska; 14, Adam Jones; 16, photo by Isabella Lucy Bird; 17, David Clay Photographer; 18, Simony; 20 Wellcome Trust; 23 Shone Atika Span; 24 Gabriel Moss; 26, PD-art; 27, Adam Jones; 28, CC-Archival Images; 33, NASA; 34, G4 im; 35,Shanghai Museum; 36, PM history; 38 Wellcome Trust; 41, jingjangjing; 47, Ggia; 49, Hirkina Makchoemi; 51, emell; 54, Aachen Cathedral Treasury; 57, Fabien Dany; 59, Dan Ruth; 60, Victoria and Albert Museum; 61, Sialkgraph; 64, Cleveland Museum of Art; 66, Detroit Institute of Art; 68, Bequest of John L. Severance; 69, Daderot; 71, Ismoom; 73, Henry Townsend; 75, Widemer Collection; 76, Wellcome; 81, Dogcow; 83, Conservatoire des Arts et Metiers; 86, 87, Mme. Pivier; 89, Smithsonian Design Museum; 91, Rob Scott; 96; Bobulous; 98, A. Heeren; 100, Daderot; 101, Wellcome Trust; 105 Derby Museum; 107, Hugo Maertens; 115, Box River Studio; 116 Stephen Walters; 117, Clem Rutter; 120, Snowmanradio; 121, 122, Smithsonian Design Museum; 123, Auckland Museum; 128 Yercaud-lango; 131, Wellcome; 134, Tim Green; 142, Jeff Kubon; 144, 145, US National Archives and Records Administration; 147, Andrew Jameson; 148, 149, US National Archive; 150, New York Public Library; 155, 159, 160, Auckland Museum; 163, US National Archives and Records; 164, Sloan Foundation; 165, Popular Science Monthly; 167, Meiji Memorial picture gallery; 168 University of Victoria Library; 171, Hiart; 173; National Archive, Netherlands; 176, McKay Savage; 177 (top), Mayondas; 177(below), Satnath;178, J.J. Harrison; 180, Peter K. Burian; 182, Charles J. Sharp; 184, Cmglee; 186, Ismoon

Preface

As Desmond Morris pointed out some years ago, human beings are basically just naked apes, and as such we lack the protection of our simian ancestors. Clothes initially did no more than protect us from the elements but in time they started to become more elaborate and decorative. As society developed and became hierarchical, clothes also became indicators of wealth and position, and no material has ever been developed that gave higher status and prestige than silk. It has been doing do for some five thousand years. That alone makes it an interesting subject to study, but there is more to it than that. It was silk that brought east and west together through trade, and along that trade route flowed ideas, technologies and religions.

I was brought up in what was then the West Riding of Yorkshire, famous as a centre for the wool industry, and as a boy went to the local school in Knaresborough. The mill down by the River Nidd was not making woollen cloth, but a finer material, linen, and we were taken there on a school visit. I found the machinery for textile manufacture fascinating – and still do. I first started researching the history of textiles for my book *Remains of a Revolution,* published in 1975, and later went on to write about the cotton industry. In working on that book and the accompanying BBC TV series, I visited India and had a chance to see a little of the exquisite work being done by craftsmen weaving silk. It, however, remained a subject of comparatively minor interest for me, until I began working on a series of documentary programmes for Discovery Channel. I was able to spend time in Lyon, visiting the excellent silk museums, workshops and factories and discovered a great deal of the history of the industry in that city. Back in the UK, I continued with visits to silk mills in Essex and Hampshire and museums in Macclesfield. The more places I visited, the more intriguing the story became.

It was in Lyon, seeing Jacquard looms at work as well as the machinery for making punched cards, that I first realized just how important this was to the whole development of technology. It was particularly striking for me, as I worked many years ago on one of the early number-crunching computers, that were fed with punched tape and at the same time was using punched cards to contain records. The more I looked into the history of silk and the Silk Road, the more interesting it became and the more it seemed that this remarkable substance produced by a rather boring looking moth had a central role in the development of so many aspects of our lives. My visit to Lyon took place more than a decade ago but that is where this book had its beginnings.

Anthony Burton
Stroud 2021

Glossary

Ahimsa silk – Indian silk produced by the wild silk moth *Bombyx Mandarina*. The moth is allowed to go through its complete life cycle, and the silk thread is obtained from the opened cocoons.

Applique – A decorative technique which, as the name implies, involves sewing a piece of fabric onto the base cloth to produce a raised motif.

Brocade – An ornate woven silk cloth in which an extra weft thread had been added above the woven cloth to give the impression the material has been embroidered. The name comes from the Italian 'Brocatto' for 'raised cloth'. It would have first been mainly manufactured on a draw loom.

Calendering – A process in which cloth is folded in half, so that the faces are in the centre. The cloth is then pressed under a roller to produce a shiny finish.

Carding – Drawing fibres through wires to align them. The technique is only used for waste silk, not for silk from unbroken cocoons.

Damask – A figured cloth which, unlike brocade, is produced with just single weft threads. The pattern is generally produced by means of a warp-faced satin weave. The name derives from the fact that the first cloths to reach Europe in this style came from Damascus.

Draw loom – The draw loom was developed to make it possible to weave elaborate patterns, by manipulating the warp. A boy perched on top of the loom, raising the appropriate healds for each pass of the shuttle.

Dressing – A combing process used to separate and align the filaments of wild silk.

Eri silk – This is similar to Ahimsa silk in that the moth is also allowed to complete its life cycle. The moth is officially known as *Samia Ricini* but gets its common name from the Assamese word 'era' meaning castor, because the moth feeds on that plant.

Figured silk – A term applied to any silk fabric with a woven pattern.

Heald or heddle – A cord with an eyelet through which the warp thread is passed. Healds are raised and lowered to create a space – the shed – through which the shuttle can pass with the weft.

Jacquard loom – Not strictly speaking a loom, but an attachment that can be added to a loom. It uses punched cards to create a pattern. When healds are activated, they can either pass through a hole in the card and be raised, or will hit solid card and remain in place. It replaced the draw boy of the draw loom. It is named after its inventor, Joseph Marie Jacquard.

Lease – A device, usually in the form of a rod, that separates the warp threads and is placed between the back roller and the healds on a loom.

Lustring – The name for a silk fabric with a shiny surface, usually produced by calendaring.

Muga silk – Silk produced from a silk moth native to Assam that has a lustrous golden colour and is hard wearing.

Mule – A spinning machine that was first developed for cotton. The threads are wound onto bobbins that go on the back of the frame, and are then passed through rollers to spindles on a moving carriage. As the carriage retreats from the frame, it draws out the threads. At the end of the run, the carriage stops and the spindles rotate to twist the thread. The carriage then returns and the threads are wound on.

Plain weave – This is the simplest weave, in which the weft threads are alternately passed over and under the warp threads.

Reeling – The process of drawing the filaments off a cocoon and winding them onto a reel / warp threads.

Sateen – A satin weave made with spun yarn instead of unbroken filaments.

Satin – Originally produced in Quanzhou in China, it was traded to the west through Arabia, where it was known as zayton. This is one of the basic weaves, in which a weft thread passes over a number of warp threads. A four-harness satin, has the weft passing over three warp threads, then under one and so on. The most pliable version is the eight-harness satin, with the weft thread passing over seven warp threads and under one.

Throstle – originally a steam powered spinning machine, based on the Arkwright water frame, in which the threads are passed through rollers, moving at different speeds, to draw out the thread, and then twisted by a rotating flyer.

Throwing – The process of twisting silk threads together after reeling.

Twill weave – One of the basic types of weave. It is created by passing the weft over two or more warp threads, and then on the next throw of the shuttle moving along by one warp thread to create a diagonal pattern.

Velvet – The weaving of velvet involves the introduction of a third thread in the warp, which forms loops. The loops are then cut to create tufts that rise above the ground fabric. This is the pile. If the pile is more than 1/8 inch high it is known as plush.

Warp and weft – The warp threads are set on the loom, running from a roller at the back of the loom to the front. The weft is the thread that passes between the warp threads, usually carried in a shuttle. An old weaving joke makes it easy to remember – the warp goes up and down, the weft from weft to wight.

Watered silk – Silk which is calendered, using grooved rollers, producing an effect rather like a watermark.

CHAPTER ONE

Bombyx Mori

On my desk in front of me is a little white cylinder, approximately 10cm long with rounded ends. It looks rather like a large capsule from a pharmacy, except that the case 'instead of being smooth' is slightly woolly to the touch. Given the title of this book, readers will probably have guessed that this is the cocoon of the domestic silk moth, *Bombyx mori*, a close relation to the wild silk moth, *Bombyx mandarina*. The cocoon is just one stage in the life of this rather dull looking creature.

The story starts with the female moth, which lays as many as 500 eggs over a period of three or four days and then dies. These are minute eggs – a hundred of them only weigh about a gram – and from these the tiny worms emerge a fortnight later with only one object in life; to eat as much mulberry leaf as they can manage, and not just any mulberry leaf. They are picky eaters and only really thrive on the white mulberry. During the next month, they will increase their weight 10,000 times. They are such voracious eaters that if you visit a silkworm farm you can actually hear the steady chomp of their tiny jaws. In that time there are four moults, in which the dark hairy larvae become smooth skinned, at first white and in the final stage slightly yellow. It is then that they begin to secrete the silk thread that wraps round the body as the cocoon, to protect the creature as it pupates. This single filament can be anything from 600 to 900 metres long. Once this stage is completed, the moth emits enzymes that attack the silk and allow the moth to escape the cocoon. The wild silk moths will fly out, but the domestic silk moth has a heavy body and can scarcely lift itself into the air, but that does not mean that they are inactive, far from it. The female emits a powerful pheromone that basically makes the males so mad for sex they will try and mate not just with the females but even with each other. Once mating has occurred, the moths soon die and the whole cycle starts again.

The wild silk moths had been following this same pattern, producing silk for their own purposes, from the time when the moth first evolved in an age long before the first humans appeared on the planet. The interesting question is this; what on earth made

anyone think that the hairy little capsules like the one on my desk had any value at all? I am reminded of the writer who argued that the existence of mayonnaise was an argument in favour of the presence of a god. Why would anyone dribble oil into egg yolks if they were not divinely inspired? The same argument can be used for silk, and in Chinese legend it was indeed a divinity who was involved.

The story goes that the discovery of silk weaving was the result of a happy accident that happened to Lady Hsi-Ling-Shih. She was the wife of the legendary Yellow Emperor, who is said to have ruled China around 2500 BCE, and as an empress she was considered at the time also to be one of the immortals. She was sipping tea under a mulberry tree when a cocoon plopped into her cup, and the silk thread began to loosen in the hot liquid. She, being a living goddess, at once understood the significance of the event and ordered her servants to turn the filament into thread,

Larvae of the silk moth *Bombyx Mori* chomping on leaves from the white mulberry tree at the Bornholm Butterfly Park.

Silkworm cocoons at a silk factory in Margilon, Uzbekistan.

and then proceeded to design a loom on which a material could be woven. We may well doubt the story, and archaeological evidence suggests that in fact silk weaving dates back even further in time. Woven silk fragments and threads found in the Zhejiang province of China have been dated to around 3000 BCE, which almost accords with the legend, but a small ivory bowl carved with a silkworm has been dated to at least a thousand years earlier. What is astonishing about these dates is that no one in the West had the least idea where silk came from or how it was produced until thousands of years later.

Whatever the date when silk production commenced, what we do know is that the development period would have been very long. The moth family Bombycidae has many wild members in many different countries, and the Chinese must have spent many generations cross breeding the wild moths to produce the domestic moth we know today, heavy, flightless and blind, which produces a fine, smooth filament. Having developed a moth that only existed to provide them with raw material, they then had to work out the best way of rearing the creatures.

The method established in China has scarcely changed over the centuries. The eggs must be kept in controlled conditions, with a starting temperature of 18°C gradually raised to 25°C. After the eggs have hatched, the baby worms are placed in trays in vertical racks and fed on hand picked mulberry leaves every hour until they form cocoons. After eight or nine days, the cocoons are then either steamed or baked to kill the pupae – if they were allowed to start emerging, they would damage the silk. When I shake my little cocoon in front of me, there is a rattle, which is the dead pupa. They are then dipped into hot water to loosen the filaments. When they emerge, the filaments are still coated with sericin, the gummy protein that held the threads together to form the cocoon. This will later be removed by washing, but at this stage the filaments are known as raw silk. This is very intensive cultivation, as it requires around 2,500 silkworms to produce a pound of raw silk. Not all the pupae were killed, some being retained to provide the next generation of breeding moths. And the broken silk that was left when the moths emerged from the cocoon was not wasted. Although it was broken into short lengths it could be used, for example, as a stuffing for padded jackets. It was to be many centuries later before anyone found a better use for it.

Chinese silk
reeling; the
cocoons have been
immersed in hot
water in the pot
to the left and the
filaments are being
drawn out by hand
and wound onto
the rotating frame.

We do not know precise details of the processes used in ancient China in creating silk fabrics, but the sequences that are required remain constant. First the continuous thread had to be unwound from the cocoon and fed on to some sort of spool. We do know that at some stage, several cocoons would have been unwound at the same time. The next step would be to twist the thread together to create yarn – the numbers of threads needed depending on how the thread was to be used in the loom, whether for warp or weft, the former requiring greater strength and therefore more twists. Reeling silk may sound quite straightforward, but in practice this was very far from being the case. No two cocoons produce threads of the same length, and the variation can be enormous – some producing a modest 300 metres, others four times as much. Care has to be taken not to take the silk from the inner part nearest the chrysalis as this is usually inferior in quality. When soaking the water has to be hot, but not too hot, or it could dissolve the silk, while hard water is liable to make the gum brittle instead of removing it. It was a task that called for some skill and a great deal of patience.

There is scant evidence of how silk was woven in the earliest times, but we do know some of the types of looms that were developed thousands of years ago. In ancient Egypt, around 3000 BC, the horizontal ground loom was in use. This consists of two parallel wooden beams, pegged to the ground, between which the warp threads are wound in a figure of eight. The warp is divided into two layers, the odd and the even. The odd threads are fastened to a stick, the 'rod heddle' above the warp. When this is lifted, it leaves a space – the 'shed' – through which the weft can be passed, either by hand or using a shuttle. The rod heddle is then lowered, and the even threads raised by means of another piece of wood, the 'shed rod' beneath the warp, to create the 'countershed'. An alternative version is the vertical warp-weighted loom. In this device, the warp is suspended from an overhead beam, and tautened by hanging weights at the bottom of the loom. Weaving uses a similar system to that used in the ground loom.

A woman weaving on a backstrap loom in Mexico.

A painted Chinese silk banner from the tomb of Lady Dai, c.108BCE. The painting shows the movement of the human soul from the earth at the bottom of the picture up to heaven at the top.

There is one other type of early loom for which there is evidence of use in China at the earliest period. This is the backstrap loom, parts of which were discovered in Yuyao in Zhejiang Province and dated as being roughly 6,500 years old. In this type of loom, one end of the warp is attached to a fixed object, such as a post or tree trunk, while the other end is wrapped round the weaver's waist. To create the shed, the weaver leans forward to slacken the threads and pulls a roller, set between the threads, towards her. To create the countershed, she leans back again to put the warp in tension and lifts the appropriate threads by means of a string. Surprisingly, this type of loom is still in use in many parts of the world to this day. The early looms produced a plain weave, but by the fifth century BCE, colour could be added by painting on the silk, either to produce works of art or to decorate material used for clothing. First the cloth was beaten against a stone to create a completely smooth surface, then the design was added using ink made of soot and glue and pigments, made from mineral such as malachite. The artists used animal-hair brushes.

One can only imagine the enthusiasm with which the first woven silk was greeted. No material like this had ever been produced before. It was light, yet warm in cool weather and cool in the heat. And it had a very special characteristic; it shimmered. As the material caught the light, so it seemed to undergo subtle changes in colour. We now understand how this happens. If you look at a silk thread under the microscope you will see that it is roughly triangular in cross section, so that the entire thread acts like an elongated prism. We know that when light is shone through a prism it is refracted and if it shines on a screen at the far side of the prism, one will see the spectrum of colours red to violet. With silk, the effect is muted but very real. This was an exotic material, and an edict was issued that only members of the royal family were allowed to wear it, though courtiers could be awarded the honour as a special mark of esteem. The emperor traditionally wore white silk inside the palace, but he, his principal wife and heir wore yellow robes when they went outside. To ensure exclusivity and to keep the secrets of silk manufacture, a law was passed forbidding anyone to reveal the details of manufacture or take the eggs out of the country on pain of death.

The ruling on imperial monopoly did not last forever, and gradually silk became more widely available. By the fifth century BCE, six provinces were involved in silk production, which was virtually all in the hands of the women. They were responsible for the tending of the silkworms, winding, spinning, dyeing and weaving. Six months of the year were devoted to this activity, and the start of the season was celebrated by the empress in person. By the time of the Han Dynasty that began in 206 BCE, silk was being produced on a wide scale. The finest silks were given as rewards to civil servants and other valued citizens. Values that had once been given in weight of gold were now using measures of silk. Taxes were paid in silk and the material now had a wide variety of uses. Beautiful paintings on silk were created and painted silks appeared in elaborate costumes. Not only did this increase production, call for the rearing of vast quantities of silk worms, but it also needed immense areas to be given over to cultivating mulberry trees, as it has been estimated that it takes a ton of the leaves to feed the silkworms and produce twelve pounds of raw silk.

Production was so widespread that the secrets of silk could not be hidden away in China for ever. It was only when the Han Dynasty began in 206 BCE that the rulers decided that it was all very well being exclusive, but a fortune was to be made by selling silk abroad – provided the secret of what it was and how it was made remained within Chinese borders. So, silk began to be traded with other countries and eventually left the great empire of the east and found its way to Rome, the equally imposing empire of the west. It intrigued everyone. It was naturally assumed that it was like very fine cotton and was

A Chinese Silk Weaver at Work in his Loom.
Printed for Carington Bowles in St. Pauls Church Yard, London.

This early illustration of a Chinese weaver, shows him working on a vertical loom, with the warp threads running from top to bottom and the shuttle is being passed through by hand.

probably grown on similar shrubs. Experts do not like to appear ignorant and baffled, so their wild guesses were bolstered by seemingly accurate descriptions of the plants and how they were processed. Pliny the Elder proved the most imaginative. He gave an elaborate account of the silk plant, how it was harvested and how the actual fibres were hairs on the backs of leaves that were removed by soaking in water. He had a few other things to say on the subject of silk as well. He did not approve. He found the sight of ladies in diaphanous silk garments morally repulsive and he was even more alarmed at the amount of gold that was leaving the country to buy the luxury. Many centuries later, Daniel Defoe used a similar argument when he railed at the importation of Indian cotton at the expense of native wool, but he knew he was fighting a battle he could never win:

> All the Kings and Parliaments that have been or shall be, cannot govern our fancies. They may make laws, and shew you the reason of those laws for your good, but two things are too ungovernable, our Passions and our Fashions.

The ladies of Rome were not very different from those of eighteenth century England; they would not, in Defoe's words, 'dress by law or clothe by Act of Parliament'. Depletion of gold reserves and balance of payments were not enough to outweigh the demands of fashion.

The more people discovered the delights of silk, the keener became the desire to wrench its secrets from the Chinese monopolists. If nothing could be learned directly, then subterfuge and cunning must do the job; it was time for some imaginative industrial espionage. Once again, the story has more than a whiff of legend.

In the fifth century, a prince of Khotan, a kingdom bordering China, wooed and won a Chinese princess. For her journey to her new home, she wore her finest clothes and jewellery, the effect completed by an elaborate coiffure – one thinks of a sort of 1960s style beehive. It needed to be piled high, because in it she concealed batches of silk eggs and cocoons. Khotan now had all that was needed to start its own silk industry but, like its mighty neighbour, saw no need to share the secrets with anyone else. The next act of subterfuge was even less likely; who would expect pious monks to be so devious?

Byzantium at the eastern end of the Mediterranean was the buffer zone between Europe and Asia. Its capital, Constantinople, now Istanbul, was a meeting place of trades and cultures. Goods flowed through, as did people, among them a Christian sect escaping persecution. The Nestorian church was founded in the sixth century and sent out pilgrims and missionaries to convert the Asian heathens. Among them were two felonious monks who made their way towards China. Dressed simply, with nothing more elaborate than bamboo walking sticks to help them on their way, they were the epitome of holy innocence. What no one knew as they headed back home was that those hollow bamboos were now stuffed with eggs. The silkworms hatched and were duly presented to the Emperor Justinian, and the Chinese monopoly was broken forever.

CHAPTER TWO

The Silk Road

The Silk Road is the name by which we know the trade route that
linked China to the west, but it is a modern term, first used by Baron
Ferdinand von Richthofen in 1877. It remains in use because it has
a romantic aura that makes it seem at once exotic and attractive.
It is, however, more than a little misleading. When we use the
word 'road' today we think of a fixed, paved route – and the Silk
Road was never that in the period which we shall be considering.
Also, we tend to associate roads with wheeled vehicles, and the
historic Silk Road was only ever used by pack animals – camels,
donkeys and horses. Nor was it a route entirely devoted to trading
in silk, though silk had a very special place in the story of the road.
Just to add to the confusion, it was never just one, well signposted
way, but had alternative routes and branches, so that it would be
more accurate to refer to Silk Roads. Nevertheless, it is a route that
was to play a vital role, not just in bringing silk to the west, but
opening Europe to new ideas and technologies developed in the
east. We tend to think of science and technology as being ideas
and techniques developed in the West and taken out to the Orient.
But for many centuries, the main traffic was all in the opposite
direction.

The traditional start of the Silk Road is Xi'an in north west China,
originally called Chang'an. It was one of the four ancient capitals
and is best known today as home of the famous terracotta warriors
museum. This was a bustling city, protected by an immense wall,
almost 27km long, completed in 190 BCE. Inside were an inner wall
and two walled markets, each covering an area of approximately
one square kilometre. The Eastern Market was mainly for domestic
trade, but the Western was the one where goods were bought
and sold by the visiting camel trains. Entrance to the market was
strictly controlled, and only officials of a certain rank were allowed
inside; not, as one might expect, only those above a certain rank.
In this case, it was the higher officials who were refused admission,
as trade was considered beneath their dignity. Once inside, these
markets were like small towns in their own right, with not just the
market stalls and shops, but also restaurants, bars and brothels,

together with warehouses where visitors could store their goods. This was a city where trade was vital to the economy.

From here, the route ran westward for 1,000 kilometres through the Gansu Corridor, squeezed between the Qinghai mountains that rise to a height of over 7,000 metres to the north and the equally inhospitable Gobi Desert to the south. This part of the route ends at Dunhuang, a town that owed its existence to a river flowing down from the hills. Here travellers had to make a decision, as in front of them lay the Taklamakan Desert. This vast region, much of which is covered with shifting sand dunes, covers an area of 337,000 square kilometres and to describe it as inhospitable is a serious understatement. There is virtually no water and the temperatures vary from a freezing -20°C in winter to a boiling 40°C in summer. Not surprisingly, the Silk Road travellers generally took a route either to skirt the area to the south or to go around to the north, taking advantage of a series of oasis towns. Sometimes, however,

One of the gateways to the ancient city of Xi'an, the starting point in China for the Silk Road.

both the northern and southern routes were impassable and the dangerous and difficult middle road through the desert was the only option. Things got no easier once the desert was left behind, for ahead lay the Pamir Knot, where the Tianshan, Karakorum, Kunlun and Hindu Kush all meet reaching a high point of just over 8,000 metres, traversed by narrow, dangerous mountain paths.

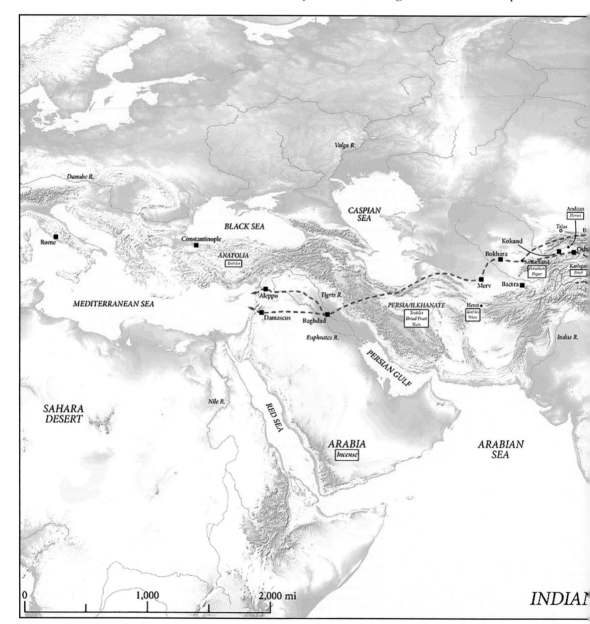

Beyond that, the way must have seemed pleasantly straightforward. The main Silk Road route continued on to Samarkand, while a second route headed south into India.

In the Han dynasty that began in 206 BCE and lasted for just over two centuries, the Chinese began securing what would become the first part of the Silk Road, from Xi'an. The earliest account describes

The UNESCO map showing the various routes taken by the Silk Road.

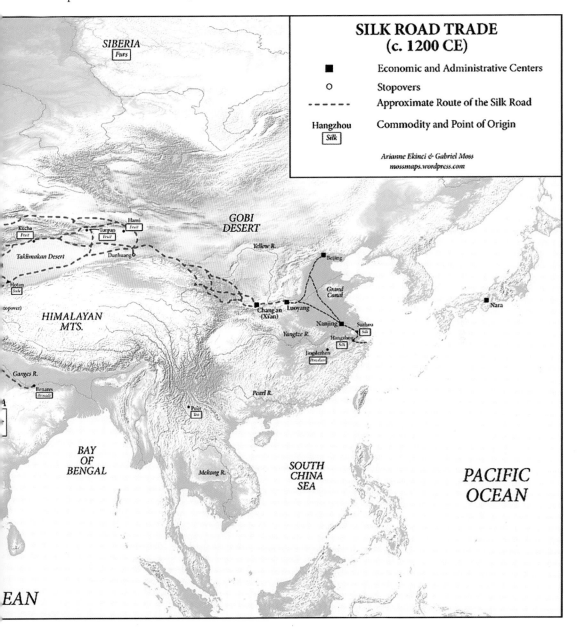

the journeys of a Chinese envoy in the second century BCE, who had been sent to Central Asia to try and persuade the Yuezlu authorities of what is now Uzbekistan to join forces against a common enemy, the Xiongnu of modern Mongolia. Unfortunately, he had to pass through the hostile Xiongnu territory and he was captured and imprisoned for ten years. He does not seem to have actually been kept under arrest, for he married a Xiongnu wife and they had a son. That seems to have mollified the local authorities, who permitted him to leave the country. Undaunted by his experience, he continued on his mission, and when he reached Bactria, an area north of the Hindu Kush, he was surprised to find Chinese goods on sale in the local markets. Clearly this was already a trade route. On his return, he was able to give the first report of the conditions in Central Asia, and it was enough to convince the Chinese that they needed to take action. In 129 BCE, an army of 40,000 cavalry made a surprise attack on the Xiongnu, inflicting a heavy defeat. This was followed by a period of warfare, which saw the Xiongnu retreating across the Gobi Desert.

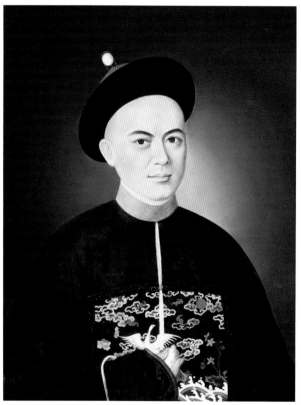

Portrait of the Chinese silk merchant Eshins, c.1800.

The Han dynastic rulers decided it was now important to secure the safety of the route and they set up a series of military posts along the Gansu corridor. They were arranged at intervals so that if trouble did occur, the soldiers in a garrison could light a beacon that would be seen by the next fort in the line. Here silk comes into the story. It was often difficult to keep these distant posts supplied and the soldiers paid. There were three acceptable currencies: coins, grain and silk. Brass coins were often in short supply; grain could rot before it got to the most distant posts so that left bolts of silk as an available and very acceptable means of payment. By this date, silk production in China had become more sophisticated and colourful dyed material as well as painted silk was available. The silk could easily be exchanged for whatever the garrisons required. Silk was indeed an acceptable currency along the Silk Road for many centuries; a standard bolt of simple, undyed silk was generally 56cm wide and 12m long. Some idea of the value can be gauged by the accounts of a Khotan Prince who exchanged 150 bolts of silk for 18 kilograms of fine jade. The posts along the Gansu Corridor were to become important, safe stopping places on the Silk Road. The whole system was carefully controlled, and travellers using the route required official passes, listing everyone who was in the caravan, and if the numbers did not match those on the passes, then they were blocked in their journey. However, the officials seem to have been trusted by the merchants. Valerie Hanson in her book *Silk Road* (2012) tells of a document that was discovered in which one merchant was complaining that he had not received a fair price for the camels he had delivered and was expecting justice.

A busy scene showing workers dyeing silk in the early years of the twentieth century. The men on the right have removed the dyed skeins and are twisting them to remove the liquid, from Arnold Wright, *Twentieth Century Impressions of Bangkok, Shanghai and other treaty Parts of China* 1908.

A modern close up view of wringing out dye as seen in the previous illustration.

A system of posts was established even earlier at the opposite end of the Silk Road. The Persian Royal Road was begun in the days of the Achaemenid Empire (500-350 BCE). It ran from the ancient city of Susa in the Zagros Mountains of northern Persia. It was here that Darius the Great built a magnificent palace that was used as the winter capital. Today it is an important archaeological site. From Susa the route went to the Mediterranean, and all along the way were posting stations, supplied with fresh horses for couriers. The system impressed Herodotus, writing in the fifth century BCE.

There is nothing in the world that travels faster than these Persian Couriers. Neither snow, nor rain, nor darkness of night prevents these couriers from completing their designated stages with utmost speed.

If these words sound familiar it is because centuries later, they were adopted as the unofficial motto of the United States Postal Service.

Details of the various routes taken in the early days of the Silk Road are difficult to come by. Documents have been recovered telling us quite a lot about the Chinese end of the route, and there are accounts of the western end, but not a great deal in between until comparatively recent times. The earliest known account of a traveller heading east was written in Greek by an anonymous Egyptian merchant, *Periplus of the Eryhthaean Sea* dating from the first century. The author describes arriving at an island off the mouth of the Ganges, beyond which 'where the sea ends somewhere on the outer fringe, there is a very great inland city called Thina from which silk floss, yarn and cloth are shipped by land.' He concludes, 'It is not easy to get to this Thina, for rarely do people come from it, and only a few.' Thina is obviously China, given the unusual name simply because there is no Greek symbol directly corresponding to the 'Ch' sound and this was the nearest approximation. We have to scroll forward many centuries to find the next useful account of travel from the Mediterranean.

Marco Polo was born in Venice in 1254. His father Niccolò was a merchant and he and his brother travelled east on a trading mission, but became embroiled in a Mongol civil war. Eventually, they arrived at the court of Khubelai Khan with whom they established a good relationship and the Mongol leader sent them back to Europe as emissaries to the Pope. Marco was then 15 years old and he was to join them on the next mission to the East, which was to last for twenty-four years. The story of those years was told in Marco Polo's book *The Travels*. The start of the journey took the family through Turkey, a country about which Marco had little to say except to note that the Turks were uneducated and spoke a 'barbarous tongue', but in the few paragraphs devoted to the country, he did note that they wove 'gorgeous and luxurious cloths of crimson silk and other colours'. And although it was never the main topic, silk weaving seems to have been noted in very many places during his journeys. They then made their way across Armenia, through the Caucasus Mountains and eventually into Persia, modern Iran. From here we can follow the travellers along one version of the Silk Road.

At the start he provided some useful information on transport on the overland route. After noting that the horses of the region were highly prized and fetched good prices in India, he then offered the slightly surprising information that the local asses were even more valuable:

> They sell for much more than the horses because they eat little, carry heavy burdens, and cover a great distance in a single day; neither horses nor mules could endure so much toil. For when the merchants of these parts travel from one region to another, they have to cross vast deserts, which is to say dry, barren, sandy regions that yield no grass or fodder suitable for horses, on top of which, the wells and freshwater springs are so far apart that long marches need to be undertaken in order for their beasts to be watered. Since no horse could endure this, the merchants only use these asses and so they fetch a better price than the horses. They also use camels, which likewise carry heavy loads and cost little to keep, though they are not as swift as the asses.

Not all the information he passed on to the readers was either that practical or, indeed, remotely credible. He described a group called the Qaraunas who raid and pillage towns and cities and do so by casting spells that turn day into night and cover the land for seven days' riding so that no one can see them coming, but they know the land so well they can rob the locals with impunity. Eventually he arrived at the Arabian Sea, from where he turned north towards Afghanistan.

At first the journey was through 'a glorious plain overflowing with things to eat' but beyond Kerman there was an arduous seven days' ride through a desert region:

> For three days there is no water to be found, or as good as none; the little there is brackish and green as meadow grass and so bitter that no one could bear to drink it. If you did drink it, a single drop would make you void your bowels more than ten times over.

He eventually made his way through the mountain passes of Afghanistan, where he described mountains so high that it took a full day to ride to the top, but where the air was so pure that people with fevers of any kind could be cured just by breathing the mountain air. Eventually, he arrived at a town he called Lop (Luobuzhuang). Here he came to the edge of the Taklamakan Desert but took a route to the south through the Lot Desert. He somewhat overestimated the size of the Taklamakan, which he described as being so large that it would take a year to cross from end to end, and a month to go from side to side. His own route was arduous enough, and he wrote that it was normal for travellers to spend a week in Lot to refresh themselves and their animals before embarking on the next stage. The main difficulty he faced was the lack of water, usually having to travel a full day and night before reaching the next supply. Often when water was found it was bitter and unpalatable. But far worse fates than thirst awaited travellers who strayed away from the main party, for they would be led away by evil spirits until they were abandoned in the heart of the desert, there to wander till they died. This is why, according to this account, travellers move together in large parties. Other authors give a more mundane reason for travelling in groups; it avoided being robbed by bandits. Marco Polo eventually crossed into China after thirty days crossing the Lot Desert.

Marco Polo's journey took him from fertile plains, through mountain passes and across deserts, and all travellers on the Silk Road would have had similar experiences. He visited many places that other travellers would have known but seems to have missed out on one of the great cities of the route. His piece on Samarkand says nothing about the place, other than it is a great city. It was indeed one of the most important places on the Silk Road outside China, though most of the magnificent buildings we see there today date from the Muslim period that began in the eighth century. Polo's main description, however, is of a miracle that occurred there. One gets a hint at the difficulties of some sections of the route, but for reliable accounts of the desert region and the difficulties encountered in crossing the mountains one has to turn to more recent accounts.

The perils of the Taklamakan were vividly demonstrated when the Swedish explorer Sven Hedin set out into the wilderness in 1895 in search of the origins of the Khotan River. He took four men with him and camels for transport, but he had seriously underestimated the amount of water the expedition needed. As the men began to collapse from thirst, Hedin set out, exhausted, to make his way, often on his hands and knees, along the course of a dried-up river bed. He eventually found water and was able to carry enough back

Samarkand, now famous for its blue-tiled buildings, was an important trading centre on the Silk Road.

to save the life of just one of his companions. Even today, with modern technology available, the crossing of the desert on foot is a slow and difficult affair. An expedition of 1993, led by the British explorer Charles Blackmore, set out, like Hedin and his men, to cross with camels. They walked for 1,400km and it took them 59 days. Part of the way was on the typical, gritty land but the sand dunes slowed everything down. Anyone who has ever tried to climb just an ordinary dune at the seaside will know what it is like to try and make progress as the sand slips away beneath one's feet, so it is hardly surprising to find that on the days in the dunes they seldom were able to travel more than 15km a day, a modest ten miles. And these were fit, well equipped men. It is hardly surprising that merchants did all they could to avoid the Taklamakan. Even when travelling round the edge of the desert, there were perils, when sudden violent sandstorms could erupt, hurling entire dunes across the paths of travellers.

The mountains offered their own challenges. At times, travellers were forced to use the narrowest of ledges high above the torrents far below them and they also needed to cross the same raging rivers on often primitive rope bridges. In some places, travellers found that even the ledges disappeared, and they had to use a series of crude steps, formed of wood or stone, driven into the cliff face. On such routes, not even pack animals could be used. A Chinese monk, Xuansang, crossed the Tianshan Mountains in 630. He described the miseries of the journey. On Mount Ling, icy pinnacles rose above the path to a height of 100 feet and some fell across the road:

A satellite image of a dust storm in Taklamakan Desert. The photograph gives a vivid image of just how barren the area is and why travellers went round rather than through it.

It is difficult to proceed on the rough, narrow paths. Add the snowy wind flying in all directions, and even fur-lined garments and boots cannot prevent a battle with the chill. Whenever one wants to sleep or eat, there is never a dry place to stop, so the only thing to do is to hang up a cauldron to cook, and to lay one's mat out on the ice and sleep.

Of the party that left with Xuansang, about a third died en route. As if the natural hazards were not daunting enough, there was always the risk of robbery. There are reports of traders losing everything they possessed – and many lost their lives. Even today, when it is possible to use paved roads to get over the mountains, the route is hazardous. Colin Thubron in his book *Shadow of the Silk Road* (2006) faced a difficult journey by Land Cruiser through the Altun mountains. It was never going to be easy as one could guess from the schedule – ten hours allowed to cover just 150 miles. In the event, it was even worse than expected; on three occasions the passengers had to get out to help dig the vehicle out of the snow and once it skidded, ending up at right angles to the road and just two yards away from a precipice. Below the snowline, they had to cope with sections of road affected by avalanches, picking their way round huge boulders and in places being forced to drive along the

A new road through the Tianshan mountains; one can imagine how difficult travel must have been before such roads were built.

bed of a stream. If that was travel in the twenty-first century, what must it have been like a thousand years earlier, before any roads were built?

Very few, if any, traders made the entire journey between the Mediterranean and China. Rather, goods were exchanged at the various stopping places along the way, so that silk woven in China might have passed through many hands before reaching Europe. Most of the trade was by barter, and Valerie Hansen quotes from documents from the market of Turfan dated 743 that give the

A figure from the Tang dynasty (618-907CE) showing a western trader on a camel.

A caravan on the Silk Road from a fourteenth century atlas.

exchange rates in terms of high, medium and low quality goods. So that, in one of these documents, horses are listed as 20/18/16 rolls of silk and camels at 33/30/27 rolls. But what is also clear is that many, many different types of material and goods were traded. The Silk Road was a passage for materials and technologies previously unknown in the west, and for new ideas and religions.

CHAPTER THREE

Invention and Innovation

Arguably the most useful and important invention to come out of China, and certainly one of the most beneficial, was the manufacture of paper. Inevitably, there is a story about how it first came about. A court eunuch, Tshai Lun, took his inspiration from watching wasps creating their papery nests. He realised that what was needed was finely chopped natural materials which, when soaked, would mat together, and when dried out would produce a material like that of the wasp's nest. He apparently used a bizarre mixture of materials; tree bark, hemp, torn up rags and fishing nets, and when he had perfected the technique, he brought the results to the emperor in 105. The emperor was delighted, praised Tshai Lun and ordered paper making to begin on a large scale. It is a good story but unfortunately, we now know that paper existed already in China at a far earlier date. In fact, the earliest fragments date back even further. A sheet of paper in the museum in Xi'an was made around 100 BCE and is believed to be the oldest surviving piece of paper in the world. The fibres used in its manufacture were from hemp and nettle.

The name 'paper' comes from 'papyrus', the plant that was used in ancient Egypt to make a writing material. Thin strips were cut from inside the plant and laid side by side, then a second layer of strips was placed on top and the two pounded together to fuse into a usable material. It was quite thick and had an uneven surface but was certainly usable as a material for writing on. As the plant's natural habitat was the Nile Delta, it was unknown in China. As a result, the earliest writing material had to make use of a local material – bamboo. Archaeologists have unearthed several documents written on bamboo strips, tied together with string to make a complete document. It appears that they were still in use after the invention of paper making, largely because the material was cheap and readily available. In fact, paper was considered so valuable, that letters and documents were reused for all kinds of purposes. For example, paper was used to make funerary garments, and papers of this sort recovered from tombs often record fascinating details. One fragment, dated to around 670, contains details of a claim by a Persian merchant for 275 bolts of silk owed to his deceased brother. The earliest fragments of paper that have been recovered were not even used for letters or documents, but as wrapping. It was inevitable, however, that eventually paper's main use would be for writing. As production techniques improved, so the price would come down and more material would become available. A valuable use for paper – that was only followed up centuries later in the West – was for money. Paper notes were in circulation in the Tang dynasty (619-907).

Paper can be made from a wide range of organic material, but the commonest method was to use rags, discarded material that would have very little other use. In fact, the use of rags in paper making continued well into the twentieth century. In Britain, the rag and bone man was a familiar figure, collecting rags for the paper maker and bones for glue. The basic technique remained unchanged. Hand made paper still uses technology familiar to the ancient Chinese. First the rags have to be cut up and mixed with water to create a pulp. A fine wire mesh is dipped into the mixture and carefully withdrawn with a layer of pulp above the mesh. It is transferred to an appropriate material, such as felt and covered

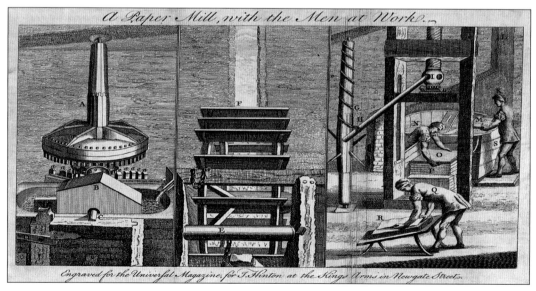

An eighteenth century paper mill. To the left is the mill that grinds up the rags with water. To the right, one man is pulling out the mould on which a sheet of paper has formed, while the other men are drying the paper and placing it in a press.

over, ready to take the next layer. The water is then pressed out and the individual sheets hung up to dry.

Paper making gradually spread west, and paper became an important commodity for trade along the Silk Road. The story of how the manufacturing methods became known in the Middle East is, like many such stories, dubious. But in this version, it all began with the attempts of the Chinese of the Tang dynasty to extend their empire westward. They were opposed by the Abbasid Caliphate and the Tibetans and the issue was decided with the defeat of the Chinese at the Battle of Talas in 751. Two Chinese prisoners revealed the secrets of paper making and a paper mill was established in Samarkand. Paper making made its way into Moorish Spain, and it is known that a paper mill was established at Toledo in 1150. The technology soon crossed the Pyrenees into France. One of the oldest surviving paper mills is the Moulin Richard de Bas at Ambert in the Auvergne, parts of which date back to the fifteenth century. It is very traditional, using a water wheel to power the machinery that chops up the rags. Otherwise everything is done by hand. Nothing here would have come as a surprise to a visitor from China travelling forward through time. The mill is the last survivor of several that were once strung out down the valley. One important Ambert mill owning family was the Montgolfiers, and if the time-travelling Chinese would have found much that was familiar he would surely have been astonished to find the paper from their mill being used to make a balloon that would carry men up into the sky. Paper had come a long way since its first use as a humble wrapping material.

Paper was a valuable commodity that was traded down the Silk Road, but its true importance depended on another Chinese invention – block printing. This was originally used for printing designs on silk, but was later adapted for printing on paper, for both text and illustration. For text, the scribe would write the words on paper, which was then glued to a block of wood. The writer would then carefully follow round the outlines, cutting through the paper into the block. This could then be inked and pressed onto paper for printing. Illustrations could either be produced in the same way or carved directly into the block. The advantage of the system is obvious; once a block has been completed, it can be used several times to create a whole series of identical pages. It can be used to make books.

The Hungarian born British archaeologist Aurel Stein made four expeditions along the Silk Road but his greatest discovery was at Dunhuang in 1907:

> In this valley there is a vast number of old Buddhist temples and priests' quarters; there are also some huge bells. At both ends of the valley north and south stand temples to the Rulers of the Heavens, and a number of shrines to other gods; the walls are painted with pictures of the Tibetan kings and their retinues. The whole of the western face of the cliff for a distance of 2 li (two thirds of a mile or one km) north and south, has been hewn and chiselled out into a number of lofty and spacious sand caves containing images and paintings of Buddha.

In these caves Stein found vast quantities of written documents, tied up in 1,050 bundles, among which was a book, known as *The Diamond Sutra.* It was produced by a Buddhist devotee and consists of seven sheets, glued together. It was dated as having been made on the 15th day of the 4th month in 868. Where other documents were hand-written, this was produced by woodblock printing, making it the world's oldest known printed book. Stein took the book and other documents away; an act which, to the western world, was essential for their preservation but to the Chinese it was simply theft. Both versions have more than a little truth to them.

The problem with the early printing was that each book had to be written by hand before the blocks could be created. The monk Zhang Tuxin, for example, set himself the task of reproducing all the essential Buddhist texts. It took him ten years. Later the Chinese were to improve on the system by developing moveable type. This was first developed in the eleventh century, using clay to form the individual characters. This is a complex business because Chinese does not have an alphabet, but instead thousands of ideograms. Nevertheless, it meant that books could be printed comparatively quickly, and as the demand for books grew, so too did the demand for paper.

Just how important these developments were becomes obvious when one considers the situation in Europe before the arrival of paper manufacturing from the Far East. Books in the Middle Ages were produced using parchment, which was created from animal skins, mainly sheep or calves. After the hair is removed, the skin is soaked to clean it and then stretched. To produce a folio of two

hundred pages required the skins of about 25 sheep. The cost of this alone made books valuable items, mainly hand-written and one-offs. Books were so rare and expensive that the great church institutions kept them in chained libraries, such as that which still survives in Hereford Cathedral. Because of the huge expense of the parchment, there was no incentive to develop printing techniques to make multiple copies in the Middle Ages. It was only with the arrival of paper and the development of printing with moveable type in the fifteenth century that book production became a large-scale operation in Europe. Yet printed books were being sold in the marketplace in Xi'an as early as 762. It had taken the West a long time to catch up, as technology moved down the trade route from China through the Muslim world to Europe. The invention of

An illustration from the Diamond Sutra, a Chinese translation of the Buddhist text produced in the Tang dynasty, and the oldest known printed book.

paper and printing are known as two of the four great inventions, of the other two, one probably saved many, many lives – the other destroyed even more.

Among the other commodities traded down the Silk Road was jade, and it was sent westward from Khotan. A less likely material was described by Marco Polo, which he called 'salamander'. The Italian traveller told his readers that a salamander was not, as they might have thought, a creature – because no creature could actually survive in a fire, but a substance mined from the earth. It was taken and pounded in a great copper vessel, then washed, forming a fibrous substance, which was then made into cloth, and then fired. The result was the fireproof material, which we now know as asbestos. In Marco Polo's time, the manufacture and trade was controlled by a lord appointed by Kublai Khan. He pointed out its value; 'I will tell you, too, that one of these cloths is now in Rome; it was sent by the Great Kahn as a precious gift, and for this reason the holy shroud of our Lord Jesus Christ is wrapped in it.' Asbestos mines can still be found at work on the southern route round the Taklamakan desert. It hardly needs saying, but mining asbestos remains a lethal occupation.

So far, we have been looking at the Silk Road as the main trading route for silk and other commodities, but there was also a considerable trade by sea and the Chinese developed the instrument that is now considered absolutely essential to navigation – the magnetic compass. The first evidence for using lodestone to point to the magnetic poles comes from the third century BCE, where it was used mainly for divination. Actual use for navigation is not mentioned until the eleventh century, when a simple compass consisted of the magnetic needle floating in a bowl of water – but that is a hundred years before the first mention of any form of compass in Europe. Unlike paper and printing, however, there is no real evidence that it was trade that brought it to the attention of Europeans. It is, however, another indication of ways in which China was ahead of the West in so many aspects of technology.

The fourth of the great inventions was gunpowder. It is first mentioned in the first century, but there are no accounts of it being used by the military until 1044, when gunpowder was used to create fire arrows. While useful materials like paper only spread slowly westward, news of new and terrifying weaponry moved far more rapidly. Once the formula for gunpowder was known, its use spread throughout Europe. There are arguments as to whether the information was passed down the Silk Road or whether it was through the warlike actions of the Mongols on the fringes of Europe. It was first described by the monk Roger Bacon in his *Opus Majus* of 1267. At this stage it seems that gunpowder was only known through Chinese firecrackers, but Bacon does list the appropriate ingredients – saltpetre, charcoal and sulphur.

The development of printed books had an immense influence on the spread of knowledge, and innovations in the Far East were to have a profound effect on the development of ideas, and on the sciences in particular. So far, we have been looking at the main line of the Silk Road as it stretched from China to the Mediterranean, but an important branch turned off south into India, where a system was developed that would revolutionize the world. The Indians invented a new system of numbers, which may not sound very exciting until one looks at the way numbers had been used in the West for centuries. The Greeks named their numbers after the letters of the alphabet with alpha the equivalent of 1, beta of 2 and so on for all 27 letters. They did not think large numbers useful, so anything over 10,000 was simply a myriad. But by far and away the most common system throughout Europe for many centuries was based on the Roman numerals. These went from I to V, X, L, C, D, M for 1, 5, 10, 50, 100, 500, 1,000, a lot less complex than the Greek 27 numerals but extremely difficult to manipulate. Alex Bellos in his highly entertaining *Alex's Adventures in Numberland* (2010) explains how Roman numbers can be manipulated. I do realise that, having written this, many readers may think the words 'highly entertaining' and 'mathematics' can hardly go together, but in this case they really do. He gives an example of how a Roman would multiply 57 and 43 – or as the Romans would have written the sum LVII and XLIII. To us it looks impossible to even know how to start. The method used would be to break the numbers down into doubles – so 57 comes out as 1 + 8 + 16+ 32. You now use doubling to get the results. So 1x43 =43. To get 8 x 43, double 43 three times and so on and add up the results, so that the only processes involved are addition and doubling. Now that's bad enough using our system, but with the Romans it looks pretty incomprehensible. This is the breakdown of 57 – LVII = XXXII + XVI + VIII + I which still looks pretty useless and the final addition of the doubles reads MCCCLXXVI + DCLXXXVIII + CCCXLIV + XLIII = MMCDLI. It is not, readers will be relieved to know, necessary to follow this through step by step let alone try and understand it or do a Roman sum for themselves. Which is why I have taken the liberty of using Alex Bellos' sum. I have quoted it at some length merely to show just how horrendously complex the Roman system is. In practice, few even tried to work out sums on paper, but relied on the abacus for calculations – and for complex calculations, including multiplications, professional abacus operators were needed. But if I was asked to multiply 57 and 43 myself using our present-day system, this would be completely straightforward, with the simple system of long multiplication I first learned in primary school. The Roman system is also counter-intuitive – the number of letters used to represent a number bear no relation to its value – so 8 is VIII but 80 is XXC. With our numerals, a number with more digits than another will always be larger – assuming of course there is no decimal point involved. That we do not mercifully have to wrestle with; this Roman system is all down to the fact we use what we call Arabic numbers, which aren't really Arabic at all. We use Indian numbers.

The Indian system was developed into its present form at some time in the seventh century. The original Indian symbols look very similar to those we now use, but the crucial point was the inclusion of the number 0. It is the 0 that enables us to move along smoothly, from 0 to 10, from 10 via 11 and eventually 99 to 100 and so on. The Indian system was carried by traders into the Islamic world, where it was rapidly adopted. Leonardo Fibonacci, an Italian whose father was a customs officer in Béjaia in modern Algeria, was impressed by the system and published a book *Liber Abaci* in 1202. He described the numbers 1 to 9 and added that 0 was known in Arabic as 'zephyr', from which we get 'zero'. Although the advantages of the system seem obvious, it was met with solid resistance. Mathematicians would not accept the idea that there could be a numeral representing nothing. All the other numbers made sense – two pigs were two pigs, but what was the point in counting no pigs? This was also the age of the Crusades, and there was suspicion of anything that came from the Islamic world. Florence actually banned their use in 1299, because it was claimed they were easy to forge. The Church also opposed their use, because of that devilish zero. Abacus professionals spoke against them for the very simple reason that they were likely to put them out of business. In fact, Indian numerals only came into general use in Europe in the seventeenth century. Of all the ideas and commodities that made their way down the Silk Road, it could be argued that none were as important as the introduction of the Indian system of numbers.

One mathematical system which did actually develop in the Arab world was algebra, the basis for which was first described in a book published in Baghdad in the ninth century. It explained the use of symbols to represent letters and used equations, such as x+ y = z, which can be manipulated, by changing one symbol to the other side and changing the sign, so that x = y-z. This was a powerful tool, which combined with Arabic numbers enabled complicated relationships in the real world to be expressed in equations. One of the most famous set of equations represent Isaac Newton's laws of motion. They can easily be used to solve problems. Here is a very simple example. You are standing by a well and you would like a rough idea how deep it is. One of Newton's equations is;

$$S = ut + \tfrac{1}{2}gt^2$$

Where s is the distance travelled, u is the initial velocity, g is the acceleration due to gravity and t is time. So all I need to do to find the depth of the well is drop in a pebble and time how long it takes before I hear it hit the water. If it was 2 seconds, then the answer is simple. There is no initial velocity; we know g is roughly 32 feet/sec/sec and t is 2 - so the answer is one half of 32 x 4, or about 64 feet. That is algebra at its simplest, but it is by working with equations of motion that physicists can work out the trajectories needed to put a satellite into orbit or land an astronaut on the moon. Modern science would not be possible without the ideas that developed along the Silk Road, nor could they be easily transmitted until they were printed on paper and distributed in books and pamphlets.

Arabic numerals were not the only devices to be attributed to that part of the world that had their origins in India. Damascus became famous for the sharpness and toughness of its swords, but their quality was dependent on a special material imported from India – Wootz steel. This was first made in Southern India in the sixth century BCE. It was generally manufactured by smelting the ore to create wrought iron, then heating the iron in sealed ceramic crucibles with organic material, plant leaves such as bamboo and beans. The wrought iron is very pure, but the crucible process introduces carbon into the iron. Modern metallurgy has shown that the carbon in Wootz steel appears as nanotubes threaded through the metal. The Wootz steel was sold as metal cakes, and it was in this form that it would have reached Damascus and the armourers. Amazingly, the secret of making crucible steel was more or less unknown in the West until it was reinvented by Benjamin Huntsman of Leeds in 1740, who slightly refined it by using charcoal instead of leaves as the organic material. His method was used at the scythe manufacturers of Abbeydale, Sheffield, which is now an important industrial museum. It had taken some 2,000 years for the West to catch up with the East. The traffic of ideas, however, was not all in one direction.

One of the most significant stopping places on the Silk Road was Samarkand, home to the Sogdian people, who had their own language and customs. The Chinese who visited them were not impressed. The monk Xuanzang, who arrived in the seventh century, described them as dishonest traders who only cared for profits. He said that when a son was born, they put honey in his mouth so that he could speak sweet words and glue on his palm so that coins would stick to it. He also said that they would go anywhere for profit, and indeed they did, for they travelled all the way to China, taking with them their own religion, Zoroastrianism. Marco Polo encountered the religion on his way to China, but merely remarked that he had come across a people who worshipped fire; Zoroastrians did have fire temples, but they did not worship fire as such. No one is certain when the religion first appeared, but it could have been as early as 1500 BCE but is more likely to be rather later. What everyone agrees is that it was first formulated by a man known variously as Zoroaster or Zarathustra.

At the heart of the religion is dualism, an endless fight between good and evil, which good will eventually and inevitably win. But it is up to individuals to make their own contribution to the fight, with the help of an omnipotent god. They were not necessarily monotheistic, but they did believe in one supreme being. Fire and water were considered as purifying elements – hence the fire temples – but dead bodies could be corrupted and could corrupt. While an essentially rational religion that places the emphasis on good deeds and truthfulness, it does have ritualistic elements of which the most obvious is the treatment of the dead. Burial was considered to contaminate the earth and cremation to corrupt the purity of fire, so bodies were exposed to scavengers on special buildings known in English as 'towers of silence'. The religion thrived in what is now Iran until the country was taken over by Islamic forces after the decisive battle of al-Qādidisiyyah in 635.

It was after this that many Zoroastrians left the country, making their way eastwards to northern India, where they established their own community, known as Parsis. They brought with them their funerary rites, so that today there are still towers of silence at Malabar Hill, Mumbai, in the heart of one of the most exclusive and expensive areas of real estate in the world. Residents have the daily sight of vultures descending to feast on human remains – which may sound disgusting to us, but it is just good, fresh meat to the vultures.

Today, the most striking buildings in Samarkand are the magnificent mosques with their stunningly beautiful decorative tiles, but there are still reminders of Zoroastrianism to be seen. In 1965, while constructing a new road, bulldozers broke the ceiling of a room that had once belonged to a wealthy merchant who in the seventh century had covered the walls with murals. One part shows a Zoroastrian priest in a face mask, and four geese, destined to be slaughtered in a religious ritual. But on other walls, the paintings show the business life of the area. Four Chinese are shown as ambassadors to King Varkhuman, bearing gifts – rolls of silk cloth, skeins of silk thread and cocoons.

If there are few traces of Zoroastrianism left in Samarkand and the surrounding area, there is ample evidence of Sogdians settling in China, in particular in the capital of the Tang dynasty, Xi'an.

A Zoroastrian tower of silence in Yazd, Iran. The dead were placed on the tower and left for carrion.

There are remains of at least five Zoroastrian temples and of towers of silence, but some Sogdians adopted Chinese burials, though the tombs were covered with Zoroastrian symbols. The tomb of An Jia, who died in 579, was discovered by archaeologists in 2001. Among the scenes depicted is one with heavily laden camels, though it is not clear whether they were trade goods or diplomatic gifts. Shi Wirkark also died in 579 and his Chinese-style tomb has a multitude of Zoroastrian symbols, such as winged horses, but the most striking illustration shows the progress of Wirkark and his wife from this life into the next world by crossing the Chinwad bridge that carries them over a raging torrent and into Paradise. The tombs also suggest that many Sogdians were moving steadily towards assimilating the Chinese lifestyle – the two tombs show the characters in Chinese dress, and although the Zoroastrian symbols are everywhere, the fact that they have opted for Chinese entombment is significant. Zoroastrianism had little impact on Chinese culture, but its appearance right along the Silk Road is significant as an indication of the movement of people and ideas.

The other great religion which would eventually travel the Silk Road was Buddhism. It originated with the son of a wealthy family, Siddhartha Gautama, in the fifth century BCE, who was to become known as the Buddha. He was moved by what he saw as the suffering of the world around him and decided to renounce his wealth and live in poverty. After a long period of abstinence and fasting he became ill and felt that this was not the answer to living a good life. He argued instead for what he called The Middle Way – neither opting for extreme poverty nor great wealth, but living life by a set of precepts, which were basically a moral code. There was no mention in his teaching of an omnipotent god, but instead there was the notion of karma or fate. In this life one should live as well as possible in the less than perfect world, and at death one would be reborn – and the nature of the rebirth would reflect the life already led. The cycle would continue until the individual reached a state of complete enlightenment, nirvana, when the cycle and suffering would end.

An essential element of Buddhism was that the doctrine should be taken as far as possible by missionary monks. It began to spread from India to the east, eventually reaching China during the Han dynasty around 50. At this period, the most important religion in the country was Confucianism which, to greatly simplify a complex subject, concentrated more on the needs of society as a whole than those of the individual, in stark contrast to Buddhism. Inevitably, it took time for the new religion to have an effect, and it was not until 178 that the first Buddhist texts were translated from Sanskrit into Chinese. It was only after the collapse of the Han dynasty in 220 that Buddhism really began to thrive. Among the more spectacular results were grottoes such as the Longmen grottoes created in the fifth century with immense statues of the Buddha. The situation changed in the Tang dynasty, 618-907, when Buddhism was attacked, with some 4,500 monasteries closed and thousands more temples destroyed. Over the years, the religion changed in China, where the Buddha came to be regarded as a god rather than merely a great teacher, but it survived and grew to the point where today China has the largest Buddhist population of any country in the world, with around 245 million followers.

There is ample physical evidence that the early missionaries from India followed the Silk Road as their main route into China. When Aurel Stein made his tortuous way through the mountains, he described finding stones with Buddhist inscriptions along the

Giant statue of the Buddha on 'Thousand Buddha Mountain', Jinan, China.

way. This must always have been a difficult route to follow, and travellers could well have been held up for long periods, waiting for the weather to improve to let them continue their journey – plenty of time to carve inscriptions to note their passage. With the opening of the Karakorum Highway in 1970, many of these stones became accessible for the first time. One of the earliest depicts a stupa, a mound containing a relic of the Buddha, which pilgrims would have walked round to show respect. It is thought that this inscription might have been made as early as the first century. Later inscriptions show the Buddha himself. It says a great deal for the zeal of these early travellers that they were prepared to undertake such a hazardous journey to bring their teachings to the wider world. Of course, not all the inscriptions need to have been made by pious monks, for many were carved by other travellers, merchants and migrants who came to China down the Silk Road.

The third religion to travel east along the Silk Road was Christianity, but not quite the religion that we know today. This was Nestorianism. In the fifth century, the patriarch of the Eastern Church, Nestorius, proclaimed a dual characteristic for Jesus, partly human and partly divine. He was at times given his divine status by God, but he was born a normal human being. Mary was no longer the Mother of God. This caused a deep schism in the church and the Nestorians were forced out of their original homeland in Turkey and settled in Persia. It was from there that they sent missionaries to the east. In the sixth century, the priest Aloban travelled to China, carrying the scriptures. Here he was received by the Taizhong who enthused over his teachings, which were 'mysterious, wonderful, full of repose'. In a Confucian temple in Xi'an, there are over 2,000 stone stelae, each of which stands around 8ft high. They record ancient texts, but among them is stele erected in 781, recording the arrival of Aloban and his doctrines. A Nestorian community did develop with its own monasteries near Xi'an but was short lived. Christianity has never had the same impact as Buddhism in China.

The fourth religion to travel east was Islam. It became firmly established in northern India, and then in China. According to tradition, Sa'd ibn Abi Waqqar, a companion of the Prophet Muhammad, visited the country with two associates between 616 and 618. There is no actual evidence for this, but it is known that Islam certainly was practiced in China in the seventh

century. Muslim merchants from the Middle East, who originally travelled down the Silk Road, and later settled in China, came to play important roles in the country. During the Song dynasty (960-1279) they regularly held an important government post as Directors of Shipping. There is still a large Muslim population in the country.

Although the style is obviously Chinese, this is, in fact, the Great Mosque at Xi'an.

CHAPTER FOUR

The Industry Moves West

India was one of the first countries to benefit from the import of Chinese silk cloth, but archaeologists have now discovered that silk was actually being woven far earlier than previously thought. Fragments were found in the Indus valley which have been dated between 2450 and 2000 BCE – just a few centuries after the first silks have been recorded in China. Investigation also showed that the silk itself came from a variety of native, wild silk moths and in many cases, the moths had been allowed to emerge from the cocoon before the filaments were unwound. Because the filaments were damaged, they could not simply be thrown and doubled, but needed to be spun. Obtaining silk in this way is far less efficient than the usual method, but because no life is killed, it was a system promulgated many centuries later by Gandhi as more humane. This type of cloth, Ahimsa silk, is still made in limited quantities in India to this day, but because it is less efficient it is necessarily more expensive and has a limited production. But in general, it seems that for centuries, wealthy Indians relied on the Chinese for their most elaborate and expensive materials. Changes came later, long after silk production had moved into the Middle East.

Silk cloth reached Europe when the Roman Empire was at its height, much to the dismay of some Roman commentators. Apparently, some silk garments were so diaphanous as to scandalise the more prudish. The Stoic philosopher, Seneca the Younger, wrote; 'I can see clothes of silk, if materials that do not hide the body nor even one's decency, can be called clothes.' He described the wives who wore such clothing as adulteresses, as any man could see what only a husband should look at. Others complained that the state was being bankrupted by the amount of silver being sent to China to pay for the luxury material. The latter is unlikely, for virtually no Roman coins have ever turned up in China. It is far more likely that the silk garments they were purchasing came from much closer to Europe, even if they originated further east. The modern names for some of these materials provide a clue. Damask is clearly a small corruption of Damascus, but satin has a less obvious origin. In fact, it indicates a type of cloth that was originally from Quanzhou in China, known in Arabic as Zayton. During the first and second centuries, it is true that most of the silk seen in Rome would have been purchased in the Arab world, but would have been woven in China, but by the second century, silk yarn was being imported and woven in the Near East, mainly in Syria and Persia.

There is some uncertainty over the question of how silk came to be woven in countries such as Syria and Persia. One version tells us that Chinese cloth was imported, unpicked into yarn and then rewoven to a new design. Another alternative is that some silk was obtained directly from a wild Assyrian silk moth, much as the Indians did with their native species. The likeliest story, however, is that yarn was imported from China, and evidence for this was found in excavations at Palmyra, the Syrian desert city which was abandoned in 273. Woven fabrics, using silk spun using a method never seen in China, were discovered. Among the materials discovered were damasks. These are reversible fabrics, usually of just one colour, in which patterns are created in the weaving process by using satin in the warp, using thrown silk and sateen in the weft, using spun silk. Because the light reflects differently from the two types, we see whichever is on top – and if the fabric is turned over, there will be the same pattern, but in reverse. This was a highly prized, luxurious cloth and only the wealthiest could afford it, usually limited to royalty.

Chinese silk thread was woven extensively in Syria at Berytos, Tyre and Antioch and the fabrics they produced often showed quite complex patterns, with animals, plants and often subjects from Greek mythology, shown in roundels. They were dense fabrics, but still gave offence – this time to Christians who objected to seeing people wearing clothes featuring pagan scenes. Under Theodosius, the last Roman emperor to rule both the eastern and western halves of the empire, weaving factories were established at Alexandria and Carthage. They were still relying on imported silk from China, but in the sixth century, things began to change. Thanks to the two monks who brought the secrets of silk to the west, cloth could be manufactured in Byzantium and could use motifs that would satisfy the most pious Christian subjects, such as the annunciation.

Silk weaving in Sassanian Iran followed a rather different path from that in the rest of the Near East. In the third century, the army of Shapur I invaded Syria, which was then under Roman control,

A Byzantine silk cloth from the so-called 'Shroud of Charlemagne', probably eighth century. It depicts a quadriga – a four horse chariot.

and took Antioch. There they took several weavers prisoner and set them to work in Khuzestan Province. Roundels continued to dominate design, but each roundel only contained a single figure. The surviving materials have been identified because rock carvings at Taq-e Boston show the Sassanian ruler Khosrau II and his courtiers all wearing robes with the same motifs as the fabrics. Appropriately, the carvings stand at one of the known stopping points for caravans on the Silk Road.

The biggest change came when the forces of Islam swept through the Middle East and into Spain and Sicily. Silk was important, as the Prophet Muhammad was a cloth merchant who especially valued silk, not just as a valuable commodity to sell, but in his personal life as well. He wore expensive silk clothes, including a red silk cloak for which he paid fifty gold dinars, and silk hangings and curtains decorated his home. Later, he would denounce red as the devil's colour, though his wife continued to wear it. After his death in 632, and the formation of the caliphate, silk factories were established under the control of the authorities. All silks had to bear the name of the caliph and the date and place of manufacture. The earliest surviving fabric, which has the roundels already familiar as motifs, was woven in the Tunis factory and carries the inscription 'The Servant of God, Marwan, Commander of the Faithful'. This could be either Marwan I who ruled from 683 to 685 or Marwan II, 744-750. In either case it is well over a thousand years old.

There were religious rules governing what could and could not be used as a decorative motif on fabrics. The issue was complicated by the fact that following the death of the Prophet, the Muslim world divided, between the Shia, those who supported the caliphate of Ali, Muhammad's son in law and his descendants, and the Suni who supported Mu'awiya, who assumed the caliphate in 661 after the assassination of Ali. To the Sunni, all representations of animals including humans were generally forbidden, though at first such designs could be used in certain fabrics, but for the Shia only the making of three-dimensional representations of living creatures was strictly banned. There were rules governing how and when motifs could be used, but in general in textiles intended for domestic use there were few restrictions. Religious rules also extended to the production and selling of silk. Two dubious sales practices were specifically banned; in one if a customer reached out and touched the cloth, he had to buy it, and in the other the dodgy merchant would throw out a roll of cloth and if the unwary customer caught it, he too would be bound to buy. The market inspector, the muhtasib, was required to act both as religious police and also as arbitrators in trade deals. In her book *Islamic Textiles* (1995), Patricia L. Baker quotes some of the rules, which although they have a basis in the Quran seem to be simply common sense, such as this one setting out the rights of the client who supplies the weaver with thread.

Thread must be received from the client by weight for weaving and the cloth returned by weight, to avoid doubt. If it is claimed by the customer that the weaver has changed thread and if he has a sample and the weaver declares it is the same, the muhtasib shall take them before persons of experience … if a man hires a weaver to weave a piece of cloth of certain dimensions and he weaves it differently … he deserves no hire.

The craftsmen in the textile industry had their own guilds to look after their interests and to organise the training of apprentices and authorising their advancement to the position of journeymen. It is indicative of the value set on elaborate decoration that the standard apprenticeship for a block maker was four years, while that for a weaver was only four months.

Islam was a unifying force throughout a vast area and instead of each region establishing and maintaining its own particular style, ideas and influences could spread with ease. Over the centuries, styles changed and designs became freer. Silk textiles appeared with highly stylised illustrations of animals and plants, but there was also a strong tendency towards purely abstract design. At some time around the end of the seventh century, the first calligraphic version of Arabic script was produced. It originated at Kufa in Iraq, hence the name Kufic for this form of writing and for centuries was the principal script used for copying the Qur'an. So, it is no surprise to find it turning up in various guises, from inscriptions on mosques in Samarkand to silk textiles. It is a beautiful and graceful form of writing, so that although the main intention might have been to include an important text, it is also highly decorative.

One of the branches of the Silk Road headed south into the Indian subcontinent. Silk was particularly prized and, as mentioned earlier, was originally imported as cloth woven in China. But during the years of the Moghul Empire, which began in 1526, but fragmented in the early eighteenth century, a period that gave India some of its most iconic buildings, such as the abandoned city of Fatahpur Sikri, the Red Fort in Delhi and, of course, the Taj Mahal. Under the Emperor Akbar the Great, royal textile workshops were established in 1572 at a number of centres, mainly in northern India. Expert weavers were brought to the new workshops from the Middle East and helped to set the pattern of development. Brocades were especially favoured, and the patterns reflected the variety of influences from Persia, China and motifs that had always been popular in India, such as the tree of life. The brocades were heavy cloths, with as many as seven layers of warp threads. Many of the cloths were almost covered in gold and silver threads and were

only available to the grandest of the court grandees. The Indian industry was able to prosper throughout the Moghul period, but over the next centuries was to suffer decline and revival as we shall see later.

Early Islamic silk cloth from the National Museum, Tehran.

The spread of Islam caused alarm in the Christian West, not merely on religious grounds; trade between the two religious groups virtually ceased. The West found itself deprived of the luxury goods it had once enjoyed. In 1095, Pope Urban II called for a crusade to support the Byzantine emperor and to send armed parties against Jerusalem. It was only the first of many such crusades, which came to be as much about plunder as piety. Silk was brought back to Europe from the East, most of which had Kufic inscriptions, which meant nothing to the Europeans. In a rather delightful irony, silk that had been stolen in the East was used to swathe the body of St. Cuthbert for interment, but no one bothered or perhaps was able to translate the inscription. So, the Christian saint was wrapped in silk with the message 'There is no God but Allah'.

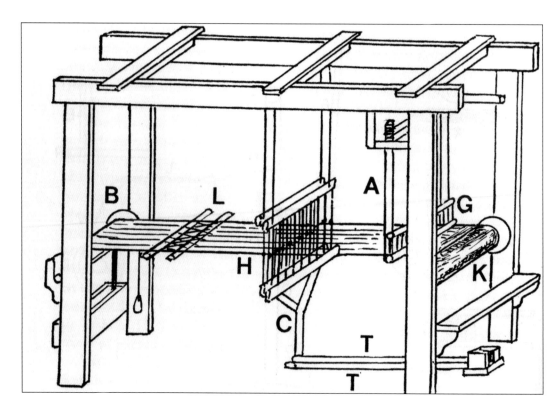

A simplified drawing of a handloom from L. Hooper, *Handloom Weaving*, 1949. See main text for details.

The technology of the industry advanced considerably in the early Islamic world. The handloom, in the basic form we still know it today, had been developed in Egypt around the second century BCE. It is worth describing it in detail as it is such a fundamental device and later improvements that followed over the years were all based on the basic model. The description given here is based on the diagram (above) which originally appeared in L. Hooper's *Handloom Weaving* (1949). It is simplified, but gains in clarity what it might lack in detail. A preliminary stage was needed before weaving could start. The warp threads had to be taken from their reels set on a frame and, if more than one colour was being used, arranged in the correct order on a roller. This was taken and set in place at the back of the loom B. The warp threads were then passed through the lease rods L. The first thread is taken over one rod and under the next, while the next is first taken under then over, the pattern repeating across the whole width of the loom. This enables the weaver easily to identify any broken threads. The threads now passed through eyelets in the healds H. These can be raised using the treadles, via the connecting rods C.

As some of the healds are lifted while others remain in place, the shed is created through which the shuttle passes. From there the individual threads are passed between the teeth of the comb G, originally made of split reeds. The comb is attached to the bottom of a swinging batten A, which is used to beat home the weft after each throw of the shuttle. The finished cloth is then wound onto the take up roller K.

Weaving material for a silk sari on a handloom in Varanasi, India.

The simplest weave is one in which plain cloth is manufactured and the same coloured threads are used for warp and weft. Where the warp and weft are different colour, the finished pattern will depend on whether warp or weft appears at the surface. More complex patterns can be created by using different colours in the warp, arranged in a predetermined pattern and by having several shuttles, each with a different coloured thread. This, of course, makes the job of weaving very complex. There are alternative ways of making patterns, using dyes. All dyes need a mordant to hold the dye in place, which in Islamic textiles was generally alum. Natural dyes, such as indigo for a deep blue and madder for red, were used. The dyeing process itself could be adapted to create patterns.

One technique in use in the early years which became very popular again in the twentieth century was tie-dying. The warp threads are tightly wrapped and then dipped into the mordant. The wrapped sections are unaffected, so only the unwrapped parts will take the dye. In the modern technique, the result is generally a series of unorganised swirls of colour in the fabric, but the system can be used to produce precise patterns. This involves painstakingly arranging the warp so that the appropriate coloured sections come together in just the right order. An alternative technique was developed in China and examples have been discovered traded down the Silk Road. In this process, layers of cloth are clamped between two carved wooden boards, with pluggable holes. Appropriate plugs are withdrawn where the pattern is required and the mordant poured through, after which the cloth goes off to be dyed. Only the sections exposed to the mordant will be coloured. The third technique, block printing, was described earlier.

One very important form of decoration was embroidery, which tends to be overlooked Yet, as Patricia L. Baker pointed out; 'From one end of the Islamic world to the other decorative stitching was used to embellish the surface of personal clothing to enormous furnishing lengths.' Male embroiders, who were paid far more than their female counterparts, regardless of skill, tended to specialise. They often worked with gold or silver wire, which, as in weaving, would be wrapped round a silk core.

A Japanese illustration of a draw loom; the man on the left is throwing the shuttle, while the man perched on top of the frame is manipulating the healds to create the pattern.

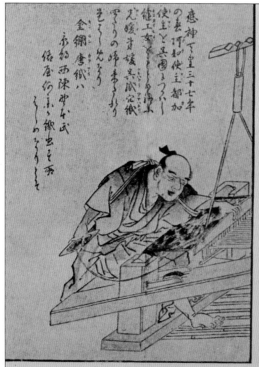

FIG. 78. — JAPANESE WEAVER BEATING-UP WEFT AND THROWING SHUTTLE

Weaving intricate patterns became far simpler and quicker with the introduction of the draw loom. No one is quite certain when it was first introduced but is usually thought to have been invented in China some time in the second century BCE, and spread from there to the Middle East. Basically, it works in precisely the same way as the loom described earlier, except that this time, the warp threads are fastened together in groups of three to six, known as lashes. An assistant sits perched on high above the loom and controls the lashes, pulling up whichever group is needed to create the pattern for each pick, or throw of the shuttle. Obviously, the order in which the lashes have to be lifted has to be worked out first and then set down as a pattern to be followed precisely. The draw loom was used in much weaving in the Islamic world and later throughout Europe and remained the most efficient way

A Persian silk brocade designed by Shah Abessi Flower in 1972, using traditional motifs.

to weave cloth with a repeating pattern right up to the beginning of the nineteenth century.

With so many options for producing elaborate patterns, Islamic silks became things of great beauty and were widely admired. Some of the finest came from Baghdad, and silk manufacturers in Spain were known to include the equivalent of 'Made in Baghdad' in their own fabrics. Even in those days, labels were important and fakes far from unknown. Inevitably, silk manufacture spread across to Western Europe, outside the Islamic world. But it seems their productions were still not as sought after as those of the Middle East. Records show that in 1670, the East India Company of London bought 2.7 million kilograms of silk from Persia. In a thousand years, it seems, standards had never dropped.

Chapter Five

Renaissance Europe

It was inevitable that such a profitable industry as silk production would move into Europe. By the ninth century, Arabic and Jewish silk artisans had started to move into Italy, but the emphasis was still very much on importing silk fabrics from the East. The city of Lucca was trading in silk, making use of its large Jewish population. One family, in particular, the Kalonymos, had kept extensive trading links with Byzantium and the Middle East. By the middle of the twelfth century, they had established an agreement with Genoa, to take goods through their territory to join the city to the port. As part of the deal, Lucca arranged for Genoese merchants to bring in materials such as raw silk from the Levant, providing the opportunity to start manufacturing for themselves, instead of simply acting as merchants. It soon became clear that manufacturing could be at least as profitable as trading and could even offer greater rewards.

By the thirteenth century, the Italian industry was beginning to thrive, though to describe it as an Italian industry is slightly misleading, since Italy did not exist as a sovereign country, but was made up of a whole series of city states; Venice at this period was not, for example, just the famous city but the Venetian Republic, and rivalry between the different regions was to be a feature of the developing industry for centuries. The first major centres to develop were in Genoa, Venice, Bologna and Lucca. Each area had its own specialities. Lucca, for example, was noted for its luxurious cloths, embellished with gold and silver threads, which were sold all over Europe and was probably by far the most successful of the silk manufacturing centres. But the industry there was greatly affected by political discord. For years, the region had been run by a 'Captain of the People', but in 1314 there was a coup and Uguccione della Faggiuoia of Pisa declared himself Lord of Lucca. He only lasted for two years before he was expelled, but in that time many Jewish silk artisans left the area to take their skills elsewhere. Some, it seems, made their way to Venice, and became an important part of the developing industry there. Initially welcomed, they were later to be treated with suspicion. In 1516, the Republic declared that all Jews must be housed in a special area that had originally been used as a waste area for dumping material from local foundries. The Italian word for 'throw away' is 'gettare' and that is the likely origin of the name given to the area in which the Jews were compelled to live – the Ghetto. Access to the rest of the city was by two bridges which were locked each night, and fines were imposed on any Jews found in the city after the gates were shut. It was the first of Europe's ghettos that were to acquire a sinister significance in the twentieth century. It was an ungrateful response to a group of people who had done a great deal to add to Venetian prosperity. Lucca itself soon returned to more profitable times and by 1371, 89 silk firms were recorded as operating and by the end of the fourteenth century, the city had an estimated 3,000 looms at work.

Venice was not the only region where Jews suffered discrimination. Sicily had an early silk industry, but it dwindled away until it was briefly revived in the fifteenth century. In 1485, Messina employed a Jewish artisan to set up a velvet manufacturing enterprise. His services were considered so valuable that some of the petty restrictions imposed on Jews were waived for the benefit of him and his family. Jewish women were required under the law to wear distinctive clothes, but his wife and family were allowed to dress as they liked. For a time, the business prospered, but then everything changed. At that time, the country was under Spanish rule and in 1492, Spain decreed that all Jews should be expelled from all their territories. Silk and politics were, it seems, closely intertwined.

A fragment of Italian silk cloth from the late fourteenth century.

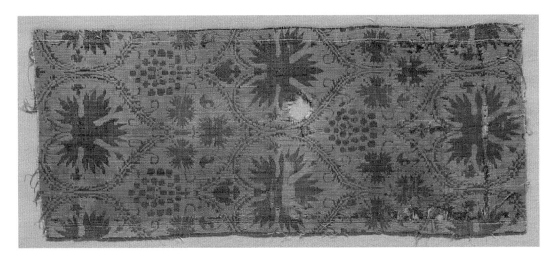

Local rulers were anxious to recruit skilled workers from wherever they could be obtained. In 1449, the Duke of Milan reached an agreement with a Florentine Pietro di Bartoli who was to try and recruit artisans from Lucca. In 1467, the Duke issued a decree that guaranteed the immigrants that their pay would be at least the equal of weavers in any of the major centres. It was successful and by 1467 there were 300 foreign workers in Milan. Other areas followed similar paths, and it was not just the workers who appeared, as they often brought their equipment with them. In his excellent book *The Silk Industry of Renaissance Venice* (2000), from which much of the information quoted in the early part of this chapter is drawn, Luca Molà quotes an entrepreneur from Modena, who explained that thanks to the immigrants, the city had 'all the necessary implements, be they water-powered spinning machines or cloth dyeing shops, while masters born in the city have learned the craft.'

The reference to water-powered spinning machines is intriguing for this is centuries before the Industrial Revolution of the eighteenth century introduced water-powered machinery for cotton spinning in Britain. Frustratingly, we know very little about the earliest of these machines, simply because the details of how they were worked were closely guarded secrets. The earliest documentary evidence comes from a Lucca document of the fourteenth century and a rough sketch from a Florentine manuscript of 1487. A much more detailed drawing was published in 1607, and it is generally assumed that the earlier throwing mill machinery must always have been similar to the seventeenth-century version. The mill machinery consists of two tall, concentric wooden frames about five metres in diameter. The outer, fixed, ring contains two rows of vertical spindles with a row of horizontal reels above them. The inner rotates about a vertical axle, turned by gearing from a waterwheel. As it moves, the laths on the inner frame rub against the spindles and reels to rotate them. Each spindle carries a fixed spool above which is an S-shaped wire. The untwisted silk passes through eyelets at both ends of the S, and as that turns, the threads are twisted together and wound onto the rotating spool. The fourteenth century document from Lucca describes the mill as having two rows of twelve reels, each reel having twelve spindles. Later mills were larger, with more spindles and reels. It seems that the mills were first developed in Lucca and were then brought to Venice and Florence. The throwing mills were the greatest Italian

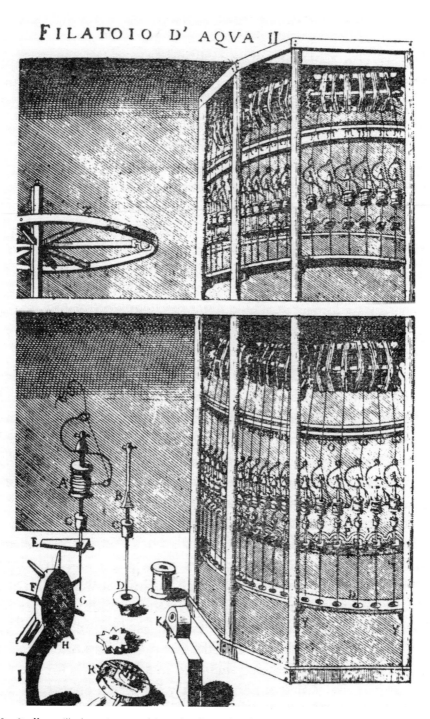

An Italian silk throwing machine, the first of its kind to be powered by a water wheel, from *Nova Teatro di Edifici et Machine* 1607.

contribution to the silk industry, and machines of similar design remained in use from the fourteenth century right through to the nineteenth.

Different areas went to great lengths to attract good workers. Many offered to cancel any debts they might have had, but the most bizarre offer was undoubtedly that made by Pope Sixtus V, who not only offered to cancel earthly debts but divine ones as well, through remission of various sins. In some cases, the foreign weavers had to be provided with suitable living accommodation. In Pisa, the authorities decided that they could enjoy a double benefit. They turfed all the prostitutes out of the city's brothels and adapted the houses for use by weavers. With so many incentives being offered to skilled workers, the industry burgeoned and as time went on, locals learned the skills imparted by the immigrants. As a result, according to a document of 1461, Florence was estimated to have one third of the population involved in silk manufacture and by the sixteenth century, there were 12,000 at work in Lucca. These figures did not necessarily include women who worked part time at doubling, warping and winding. A very good indicator of just how the industry had grown can be gauged by a report from the Venetian ambassador to Florence, who noted that the region was importing 400 bales of silk, roughly 70,000kg a year.

A report from Verona to the Venetian authorities, pointed out just how useful bringing in workers for the industry was for the whole development of an area:

'Since the art of black velvet has many crafts in it; some of them are suitable for women and children, such as raising silkworms, reeling and winding silk; some are for more mature men, such as sorting silk, dressing it, dyeing it. Some are for merchants, such as running shops, trafficking in currency, bartering and selling; some are for citizens, such as planting, making working shops with merchants and producing cloths.'

The writer then went on to produce what must have been the clinching argument in favour of starting the industry; it would increase tax revenue.

Velvets were an important and valuable commodity. They were made by adding an extra warp over a series of small rods, forming small loops which could then be cut or left as loops before the rods were removed. Velvet is still made on handlooms using this

A portrait of Eleanor of Toledo (1503-72), the wife of Cosimo de Medici, wearing an Italian silk velvet dress.

technique in Lyon, where I watched a weaver at work in his atelier at the back of a specialist silk shop. There are many variations, with mixtures of cut and uncut pile. Piles can be placed one on top of the other to create patterns, and supplementary threads can also be added to make brocades. These were luxury cloths, commanding a high price, and could only be afforded by the wealthiest and most important members of society. In Venice, for example, most noblemen dressed in black, but officials of the Senate had to wear coloured garments, each official having his position specified by a particular colour. Needless to say, they were not content with wearing a plain coloured cloth but favoured elaborate brocaded velvets.

Entrepreneurs who wanted to make a fortune by setting up businesses in other parts did not always have an easy time. In 1537, Antonio Guidotti went to England and settled in Southampton as a merchant but had to beat a hasty retreat to avoid being gaoled for bankruptcy. Then he saw an opportunity to return to Britain to set up a silk business that would repay his debts and still produce a handsome profit. He corresponded with Thomas Cromwell, a Privy Councillor and holder of many official offices. He received encouragement, and no doubt also hoped for a subsidy, as he stressed how much the enterprise was costing him. He employed a Florentine weaver, who recruited a workforce of twenty-four skilled men, together with their equipment. They duly set sail for Southampton, but there is no record of them ever arriving in Britain. Some entrepreneurs fared even worse.

Two brothers, Luca and Nicolo, surnames unknown, arrived in Italy from Ragusa, a republic in Dalmatia, the area around

Dubrovnik. Luca persuaded a young velvet weaver in Venice to join him in the enterprise. He in turn found recruits among his friends – two more weavers, a dyer and a spinner. They then paid for the construction of machinery for spinning and throwing and bought looms and dyed silk. Under Venetian law, it was strictly forbidden to take these workers and their machinery out of the Republic, but they hoped to get away with it, by hiring a vessel to take them only as far as the island of Curzola in the Adriatic, which regularly traded with Venice. Then they planned to move on to Ragusa on a second ship. Unfortunately, with so many people involved, news of what they planned was leaked to the authorities. They were preparing to leave when the harbour authorities swooped, confiscating all the equipment.

Having poached workers from other areas, each region introduced punitive laws to try to prevent the same thing happening to their newly acquired work force. Most laws simply prohibited movement of workers and specialist machinery, offences usually

Venetian Procurator's stole of the sixteenth century, which was worn over the shoulder as a badge of office. The cloth was woven to create two stoles, hence the seam down the middle.

accompanied by large fines, but which might include imprisonment for a short time. Others were altogether more draconian; an edict of 1314 offered a bounty to anyone who murdered an émigré worker. The lengths to which authorities would go was exemplified by a major row that developed between Florence and Siena. The latter decided it needed to join the silk bonanza and did as everyone else had done, bribed workers from nearby Florence to come to their city. The Florentines responded by sending agents to bribe them to come back again, adding they would be especially welcomed if they burned down the workshops and looms before they left. Then Siena responded by passing a law that stated that any agent attempting to bribe workers to leave Siena would be publicly flogged, branded on the face with a red hot iron and on top of all that pay a fine as well. One can safely assume that agents were suitably deterred.

The laws were never really effective, and in time silk workers moved freely throughout Italy. In the middle of the sixteenth century, a merchant gave evidence to the Council of Verona:

> In the past I organised the production of velvets in the city of Mantua and master artisans came to work there from Genoa, Milan, Bologna, Ferrare and all the other cities of Italy, and they worked for me, three, four, six months more or less depending on their wish.

It was clear that movement was no longer controlled, as silk manufacture spread out from Italy to other parts of Europe.

France was among the first beneficiaries of Italian expertise, and an industry was soon developed in Tours. The city had been, for a time, capital of France and still had a royal palace, used by the court. Royalty, aristocracy and the church were the main customers for the most expensive silks, so Tours was an ideal centre and enjoyed royal patronage under Louis XI. Having established workshops in Tours, the king decided to set up another in Lyon, which he expected the locals to pay for. The merchants of Lyon were less than enthralled by the idea, as they were doing very nicely indeed importing expensive silks from Italy and the last thing they needed was home grown competition. So, for a time, Tours was the main centre for silk manufacture in France. In 1546, the Venetian ambassador, Marino Cavalli, reported that several master craftsmen had settled in Tours with their families, and were teaching the intricacies of fine silk weaving to French workers.

French silk dress and petticoat c. 1760, on display at the Museum of Fine Arts, Boston.

In 1536, a Piedmontese entrepreneur, Stefano Torchetto, was granted letters patent by Francis I to set up silk industries in 'Avignon, Genoa and other places' but the biggest change came during the reign of Louis XIV who gave orders to Jean-Baptiste Colbert, the Minister of Finance, to reorganise the French industry. By this time, Lyon, having originally rejected the whole idea of manufacture, had already had a change of heart. And it was Lyon that Colbert chose to be the main centre of development, and by the late eighteenth century there were estimated to be 15,000 working in the industry. Lyon became the most important manufacturer of silk in the whole country, a position it holds to this day. The Silk Museum in the city shows some of the magnificent cloths produced for the court at that time, including an elaborate dress created for Marie Antoinette, though given that lady's ultimate fate, it seems a little tactless to display it on a headless model.

Other centres produced a variety of different silks. Tours became known for ribbed silk – 'gros de Tours'. Paris, Nimes and Avignon produced plain silks that could be bought by the wealthier middle classes. Lesley Miller, in her article on French silks (1650-1800) in Jennifer Harris (ed) *5,000 Years of Textiles* (1993), quotes prices for different types of silk in the middle of the eighteenth century, which illustrate the vast difference in prices, ranging from retail process of 180 to 350*l*- per ell for very rich brocaded silks, decorated in gold and silver, to 2 to 14*l*- for plain silks. The advantage to the merchants of opting for the richest materials becomes clear when one looks at the prices paid to the weavers. The maximum paid to a weaver of the richest and most elaborate brocades – the ones that could be sold for as much as 360*l*- was only 36*l*- per ell, but the profit margins dropped sharply for the plain cloths. The rates paid to weavers were not very different from those for the artisans making brocades, but the price the cloth could be sold for was only a fraction of that for the elaborate varieties. It obviously paid to specialise in the most expensive silks, but that depended on having a large enough demand – and enough customers who could afford the high prices. Fortunately, it seems that throughout Europe, silk was the must-have material for royalty and aristocracy. In Britain, William Lee invented the stocking frame for knitting stockings in the 1580s. He hoped to receive royal patronage and Elizabeth I was said to have been initially enthusiastic. Then she was told it could not be used for silk stockings and her interest evaporated on the instant.

Various patterns were adopted at different periods as fashions changed. Basically, there were two types of design – point repeats and comber repeats. The former were symmetrical along the length of the cloth, and were mostly preferred for furnishings. The combers were not symmetrical at all, which gave the designers freedom to produce ever more extravagant dress fabrics. These were designs that came to be known as bizarre, which does not in this context mean odd so much as very elaborate without obvious repeating motifs. By the middle of the eighteenth century, there was a trend towards painted and printed silks, rather than purely woven. But whatever the motifs and styles that came into vogue, the silk masters had no option other than to follow the trend. One valuable customer, however, continued to demand rich vestments – the Catholic Church. But towards the end of the century, all this huge extravagance and show became too much for the population as a whole. The French Revolution brought it all to a sudden and

The exquisite detailing of a French court dress from Lyon, c. 1750, decorated with silver wrapped yarn, on the Musée de Tissus, Lyon.

dramatic end, and the demand for beautiful silks died alongside its aristocratic patrons.

One textile that was of huge importance throughout the Middle Ages and the Renaissance was tapestry. The houses and castles of the nobility may have looked grandly imposing, but they were also likely to be cold and draughty, so wall hangings had a very practical purpose. But they also became works of art in their own right, and nobles often took their own tapestries with them when they travelled, for they were marks of prestige. The English king Henry VIII had a vast number of tapestries and one set of ten that he commissioned were valued a century after his death at around £5,000 – over £500,000 in today's currency. This was an expensive business. One of the early and most famous centres was Arras in northern France, a city with an extensive woollen trade. Its tapestries were so famous, that the name of the city became synonymous with the product – which is why, when Hamlet stabbed the unfortunate Polonius, Shakespeare called the wall hanging behind which he was hiding an arras. The earliest tapestries were made exclusively of wool, but as time went on, the more beautiful designs began to call for the richness of silk.

In France, Jean-Baptiste Colbert, who had helped establish Lyon as a silk centre, now set about reorganising the tapestry ateliers of Paris into one great site at the Gobelins workshops in the city beside the River Bièvre. The name would become synonymous with some of the finest tapestries ever produced. Under the direction of Charles le Brun, it produced masterpieces for the royal court, many of them featuring stories aggrandising the king, Louis XIV.

Strictly speaking, tapestry can be defined as any woven pictorial fabric and dates back to ancient times – tapestries were most famously found in the tomb of Tutankhamun. But in this chapter, we are looking at how they were made in Europe from the Middle Ages. The starting point is the cartoon – not a funny drawing, but the painted design that would be copied by the weavers. Among the famous artists who produced these cartoons was Raphael. In 1515, he was commissioned by Pope Leo X to produce full-scale designs for sixteen tapestries showing the lives of St. Peter and St. Paul which were to hang in the Sistine Chapel in Rome. Seven of the original cartoons are now part of the British royal collection and are displayed in the Victoria and Albert Museum in London. One of the greatest of French cartoonists was Francois Boucher, who worked at Beauvais originally, but was made director at

A sixteenth century French tapestry showing Daphne choosing Diana as her ideal in the Virginia Museum of Fine Arts.

Gobelins in 1755. His speciality was the romantic, pastoral idyll, in which lovesick swains seldom seem to have anything much to do apart from serenading swooning milkmaids in the shade of a tree. The Royal Court loved them and they fitted perfectly with the taste of the time – this was the age when Marie Antoinette could spend a fortune setting up an idealised 'farm' where she and her companions could dress as milkmaids and shepherdesses – though it is highly unlikely that any cow was milked or any sheep shorn by them. They were Boucher figures in a Boucher farm. It is no wonder that the famous encyclopaedist Diderot wrote of Boucher – 'That man can do anything – except tell the truth.' But they make lovely pictures and beautiful tapestries.

Two types of loom were used, the vertical and the horizontal. In both cases, the weaver worked at the back of the warp. With the vertical warp loom, the annotated cartoon hangs on the wall, behind the weavings alongside a mirror that allows the weaver to check that the front of the tapestry is proceeding as it should by direct comparison with the cartoon. With extremely large cartoons, they might be cut into pieces, and a number of weavers would be employed, each copying his own section. Examples of this type of

A tapestry based on a design by François Boucher made at the Beauvais factory c. 1750. Woven with a wool warp and silk weft it depicts the Dream of Ronaldo.

working can be seen in the Victoria and Albert Museum in London, where seven Raphael cartoons were cut up in this way but have now been reassembled and put on display. With the horizontal loom, the arrangement is similar, except that the cartoon and mirror are on the floor. Large numbers of weft threads are used, and many weavers can work at the same time on the same tapestry, which was just as well as with a complex design a single weaver could only produce about one square metre a month. To put that in perspective, the Raphael cartoons mentioned above are roughly fifteen square metres – each one would have taken well over a year for a single weaver.

Tapestry weaving was not perhaps the most important use of silk in terms of quantity of thread used, but the end products stand among the most beautiful creations that used the material. But by the end of the

Tapestry weaving at the Gobelin works in France in the eighteenth century.

eighteenth century, the demand for tapestries had all but disappeared while the market for material for clothing and furnishings continued to grow – everywhere that is except in Revolutionary France, where such fripperies were well and truly out of favour. When the French industry revived in the early years of the nineteenth century, it brought with it a major change in production technology that would have profound implications and began a process which has changed our world forever. But before turning to that subject, there is one other contribution to the modern world in which silk played a part from the start, and it is a rather surprising one: aviation.

At the end of the eighteenth century, Joseph Montgolfier became obsessed with the idea that it would be possible to move armies by air using balloons. In particular, he thought the siege of the British garrison at Gibraltar by the French and Spanish could be brought to a swift end if the French could land on the Rock from the air. According to legend, he got the idea when a chemise that was drying before an open fire was caught by the updraft of warm air and rose to the ceiling. The story has probably as much truth as most such legends have; very little. He did, however, realise that a balloon could be lifted into the sky, by burning material underneath it, though he seems to have thought there was something in the nature of the materials used in the fire that caused the effect; he favoured a mixture of chopped wood and sheep's wool as the fuel. In 1782, he made his first hot air balloon, an envelope of silk with a hole at the bottom, which he demonstrated to his brother Étienne, who was greatly impressed and proposed making a far larger balloon. The Montgolfiers went on to build far more balloons and in September 1783 the first aeronauts took to the skies from the Palace of Versailles, watched by Louis XVI and Marie Antoinette; not daring humans, but a sheep, a duck and a cockerel who landed safely after a flight of three kilometres.

The Montgolfier brothers were not the only early experimenters. They inspired another Frenchman, Jacques Charles, with his brothers Ainé and Cadet, to try an alternative to hot air as a lifting agent. They used the lightest gas, hydrogen. Their biggest problem was how to prevent the hydrogen escaping through the fabric. It needed to be light but impermeable, and like Joseph Montgolfier they turned to the fine material, silk, but coated it with rubber solution. The hot air and the hydrogen balloon, the latter later developed into the airship, were to be the only means available for flight until the Wright brothers' heavier than air craft made its first appearance over a century later. Silk had been the first

FIGURE EXACTE   ET PROPORTIONS.

DU GLOBE   AËROSTATIQUE,

Qui, le premier,   a enlevé

des Hommes   dans les Airs.

The Montgolfier brothers were pioneers who created the first hot air balloons; their first balloon was made of silk. This later version was silk and paper.

material to be used, and the fabric was to appear again in another major advance. In October 1797, an enthusiastic French balloonist, André-Jacques Garderin, went up in a balloon with a new device above the gondola, what looked like a huge umbrella. It was, in fact, a silk parachute. When he had reached a good height, he cut the rope attaching the gondola to the balloon, unfurled his parachute and descended safely, if somewhat erratically, to land. Once again, silk had proved its versatility, but now it is time to turn away from aviation and back to the world of high fashion.

CHAPTER SIX

Automation

The draw loom was a great success in its time but suffered from one serious disadvantage. It required the vigilance of the draw boy – and it usually was a boy who could fit himself on to the top of the loom – to pull up the appropriate warp threads for each pass of the shuttle. It required a great deal of concentration to follow the correct sequence that would produce the pattern, which would normally be indicated in diagrammatic form. It was a system that could be improved by some form of automation. The first to attempt the job was a Lyon worker in the silk industry, Basile Bouchon. His father was an organ maker, so Bouchon could see a form of automation in the barrel organs he produced. In these organs, a tune is produced by means of pins and staples arranged on the barrel – pins for short notes, staples for long. As the barrel is turned, the pins engage with the valves that allow the air into a particular pipe. Each barrel contains just one tune, the unique arrangement of the barrel corresponding with the notes required. For an organ to work well, the pins had to be positioned with extreme accuracy, and the normal practice was to punch holes in paper for the correct design, then wrap that round the barrel – holes would then be drilled into the barrel corresponding with those of the paper. This was the inspiration for Bouchon's semi-automated loom of 1725.

In the Bouchon loom, as in the barrel organ, a pattern of punched holes was created in a paper that was wrapped around a perforated cylinder. A series of hooks attached to needles were arranged in a box at the side of the loom so that each hook could snag a string that would lift a warp thread. When the cylinder was pushed towards the box, if the needle met an unperforated section of paper, it would be raised, lifting the thread. If the hook met a hole, then it simply passed inside the cylinder. The cylinder had to be rotated by hand for each throw of the shuttle, and was partially successful, but not widely adopted. There were two problems. Firstly, it still required a boy to operate the device, so there was no saving in labour costs. Secondly, paper is fragile and easily torn. Any tear would mean that it would have to be taken away for repair or even

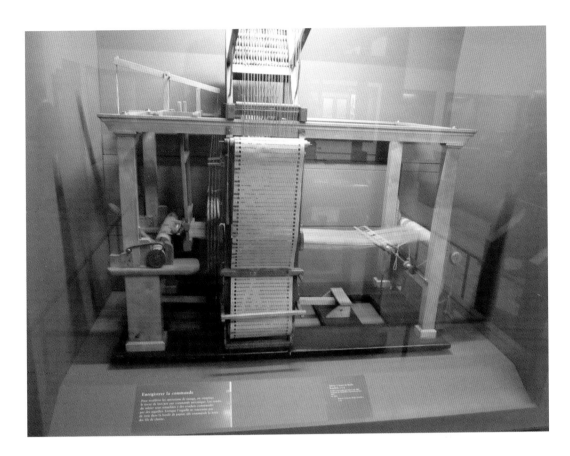

used as a template to create a new punched roll. There was also a limit to the number of threads that could be handled, making it useless for the most complex problems. In 1728, one of Bouchon's assistants, Falcon, made a major improvement. He replaced paper with punched cards and increased the number of warp threads that could be lifted by arranging the holes in rows. It got over one of the problems – a fault on one card just meant that just that card had to be replaced, not the whole roll. It is thought that around forty looms of this type were sold altogether, which is a minute proportion of the thousands then in use.

In 1741, Louis XV's Chief Minister Cardinal Fleury was given the task of looking for ways of improving productivity and creativity in the French silk industry that was now showing signs of falling behind other European countries. One might have expected him to appoint someone with a detailed knowledge of textile technology as an inspector, but instead he chose Jacques Vaucanson, who had been born at Grenoble, the son of a glover. Although he had no

The Bouchon loom that used perforated paper to control the movement of the headless. This version is in the Musée des Arts et Metiers, Paris.

experience in textiles, Vaucanson had acquired a reputation as a remarkably ingenious designer of automata. One suspects that the cardinal might have been an acute man who recognised that the future lay with automation and the fresh eye of a genius mechanical inventor might be more useful than an expert steeped in tradition. At the age of just 18, Vaucanson created his first machines, androids which could clear the table and serve guests at a dinner. That was just the start. His next ambitious project was a full-sized figure of a flute-playing shepherd with a repertoire of twelve songs. But his most celebrated creation was the Digesting Duck. The automaton had hundreds of moving parts – the life-sized duck could flap its wings, quack and 'drink' water. The feature that gave it the odd name was totally bizarre. The duck could be fed pellets of food and after a short time, a little squirt of all too realistic green slimy poo would appear from its backside. After that, automating a loom might have seemed quite a minor problem.

Vaucanson took the ideas developed by Bouchon and Falcon and improved on them by making the loom self-acting. He moved the mechanism to the top of the loom, so that it could act directly on lifting the appropriate threads by the same system of needles, hooks and punched cards. The mechanism however depended on a complicated sliding cylinder. There is no evidence that the loom was ever adopted – and some experts have suggested that it might well have been unworkable. It did, however, pave the way for the real breakthrough.

The next inventor to tackle the problem was Joseph Marie Jacquard. There is a certain amount of confusion about his early life, beginning with his name. He was, in fact, called Joseph Marie Charles, but there were several related Charles families all living in the same district, so to distinguish them from one another they all had nicknames – this branch was Jacquard and the name stuck. He was born in 1752, the son of a master weaver, and one of nine children, only two of whom survived. He never received any formal schooling and remained illiterate until the age of thirteen, when he was helped out by his brother-in-law, a printer and bookseller. He also introduced Joseph to a circle of intellectuals, and it seems that although intellectually astute, he was physically quite delicate. Inevitably, he started his working life with his father at the loom, but when that proved too much for him, he too moved into bookbinding and printing. When his father died in 1772, he inherited the estate which, as well as the

textile workshop, included a vineyard and a quarry. By 1778, he was referring to himself as a master weaver and silk merchant, which suggests that the family inheritance gave him a degree of independence rare among weavers. The family income increased when he married a widow, Claudine Bouchon, who brought with her property and a substantial dowry and they had a son in 1779. The prospects must have looked good, but he fell into debt and had to sell off his father's inheritance. However, he continued in business and began attempts to automate the draw loom, with limited success.

The Vaucanson loom improved on the Bouchon by using punched cards instead of perforated paper.

A portrait of Jacques Marie Jacquard woven in silk on a Jacquard loom.

The French Revolution had, of course, a profound effect on the silk industry and, in 1793, there was an uprising against the extremists of the Convention. Jacquard and his son sided with the rebels. But when it became obvious the cause was lost, they fled the city. Their position could have been serious, but they took pseudonyms and went for the one place they knew they should be safe; they both joined the Revolutionary army, fighting in the Rhine campaign, during which, tragically, Jacquard's son was killed. When he returned to Lyon, he seems to have taken a whole variety of different jobs, from repairing looms to bleaching straw hats. Then, somewhere around 1799, he turned again to invention. The results were a treadle loom that he patented in 1800 and a loom for making fishing nets. He was again working on automating the draw loom, which he developed in 1801.

He showed the loom at the exhibition of French industrial products in Paris in 1801, where he was awarded the bronze medal. In 1803, he was called back to Paris and while there had a chance to see a Vaucanson loom at the Conservatoire des Arts et Metiers. By 1804, he had his own device perfected. He now showed the device in Lyon, where it received a very different reception.

The story of the Industrial Revolution in Europe is one of violent reaction to labour-saving devices. In Britain, when Sir Richard Arkwright attempted to open one of his water powered cotton mills in Lancashire, it was burned to the ground. The introduction of machines for dressing cloth in Yorkshire were smashed by Luddites. It is not difficult to see why. Merchants and manufacturers saw their costs cut and profits increase, but skilled craftsmen saw their livelihoods threatened as the machines took over their crafts. In Lyon, there was the same fear. If machinery could be used to create complex patterns, their specialist skills might no longer be needed. On top of that, many families relied on the income from the draw boys, whom the Jacquard machinery would make superfluous. His new machinery was smashed. But ideas are not as easily destroyed as machinery.

1804 was not just the year that Jacquard unveiled his invention, it was also the year Napoleon was declared Emperor. The austerity of the Revolution was rapidly abandoned and the new court was to prove as avid for silk as the old had been. The new administration was also keen to promote inventions – the old enemy across the Channel had been making huge strides in industrial progress, and Napoleon had no intention of seeing France lag behind. Jacquard was summoned to Paris, where he had a two-hour interview with the emperor, in which he explained the principles of his machine. Napoleon was impressed and Jacquard was given an apartment and workshop at the Conservatoire des Arts et Metiers in Paris, together with a handsome allowance that left him free to concentrate on perfecting the machine.

The Jacquard mechanism used a continuous chain of punched cards, wrapped round a square box. As each card was put in place, a simple treadle was used to raise rods attached to hooks. Rods coinciding with holes, remained unmoved, while those meeting solid card were displaced. A beam then rose up and connected with the rods that had been left in place. Threads from the hooks were attached to one or more headles, which would then be raised to make the shed. The great advantage of the system was that it did not require a second person to work at the loom and it offered a way to reproduce even the most intricate patterns. Although the device is usually known as a Jacquard loom, it is really a Jacquard machine that could, in theory, be used with any loom. The only disadvantage is that it added greatly to the height of the whole system, and some workshops were unable to fit them in – and, of course, there were always those weavers who could not afford the expense.

An essential part of the operation was the creation of the cards. The design had first to be drawn out on squared paper and the pattern transferred to the cards. An early version in La Maison des Canuts in Lyon starts with the warp threads to be used in the design arranged in the correct order on a vertical frame. The operative takes each row of the design at a time and pulls on the appropriate threads to create a template. This then goes to a more elaborate machine that punches the holes, and finally a third machine is used

A Jacquard loom of 1810 in the Musée des Arts et Metiers, Paris.

A close up view of the punched cards of a Jacquard loom; the changing pattern of holes indicate which headless are to be lifted and which will remain in place.

to sew the cards together in the correct order, in a continuous loop. Once a pattern has been completed, and the loop has come full circle, the next pattern can begin to be formed. An alternative can be seen in Macclesfield, which uses a machine not unlike a typewriter keyboard to punch the holes manually.

In spite of the opposition of the Lyon weavers, the Jacquards spread rapidly throughout France, and Napoleon himself was one of the beneficiaries. Some of the exotic fabrics he acquired can be seen in the Musée des Tissus, also in Lyon. It was estimated that a skilled weaver working on an unadapted draw loom could produce one inch of highly decorated silk a day; with the addition of a Jacquard he could weave two feet. There are not many machines that can instantly produce a 1,200 per cent increase in productivity, so it was inevitable that news of such a device soon spread outside France. Stephen Wilson of Lee Wilson & Co. of Spitalfields sent an industrial spy to France who reported back in a letter of 1820 that he had seen the whole operation and was sneaking a card, rod and hook out of the country.

One huge advantage of the Jacquard mechanism was that it could be applied to almost any loom, and by the start of the nineteenth century, power looms were starting to come into use. The story of the development of the first successful power loom did not come directly from the silk industry, but it is worth telling simply because it is so bizarre. The Reverend Edmund Cartwright was the rector of Melton Mowbray, a town better known for pork pies than textiles. Indeed, Cartwright had never even seen a weaver at work when he was told by a Manchester manufacturer that it would never be possible to mechanise the handlooms. He decided to prove the expert wrong and set about designing a power loom, eventually producing a model that he patented in 1786. It was not a huge success. The warp threads were vertical and, in the inventor's own words, 'the reed fell with the weight of at least half a hundredweight, and the springs which threw the shuttle were strong enough to have thrown a Congreve rocket'. The Congreve rocket was a military rocket, which could carry an explosive load of several hundred pounds, which gives some idea of the force needed for Cartwright's shuttle mechanism. Originally, the power source was two strong men – who were exhausted after about an hour. He went on to make further improvements and took out more patents. In its final version, the shuttle was thrown using a combination of levers and cams, powered not by exhausted helpers but by waterwheel or steam engine. Later improvements were devices that automatically stopped the machine when a weft broke, or the shuttle got jammed. With these improvements in place, a weaver no longer had to concentrate on just the one machine to instantly deal with any problem but could tend two or three looms. Not only did handloom weavers find themselves increasingly displaced as the work moved from home and workshop to factory, but the new looms were now often worked by women instead of men. The textile world was changing, and the changes affected all branches including silk.

The Jacquard revolutionised silk production, but the basic idea of controlling complex actions through punched cards was to have far reaching consequences. At the heart of the whole machine was the card with punched holes. It is rather satisfying to think that one

A promotional silk panel showing the heraldic lion of Lyon and a train taking goods all over Europe while the ship sails off to America.

use goes right back to Bouchon's original inspiration, the barrel organ. The rotating barrel was quite a crude arrangement, and each barrel could only play one tune. In the nineteenth century, the magnificent fairground organ was produced. The traditional church organ is supplied with a continuous supply of air, and when the organist depresses a key on the console or pulls out a stop, it opens a valve allowing the air into one specific pipe producing a particular note. It is not difficult to see that a Jacquard type of card could be used – where holes in the card permit air to go to the appropriate pipe. It is necessarily complex, as the fairground organ was designed to produce a sound like a band – so some pipes would produce a trumpet like effect, while others would be fitted with reeds to imitate, for example, a clarinet. And, of course, for each 'instrument' a whole range of notes would have to be provided. I recently visited the Dean family workshop near Bristol, where they make and repair fairground organs, and discovered that one part of the manufacturing process has still not been automated; the cards are still cut by hand. The holes, unlike those of a Jacquard, are rectangular, and the length of the slit determines the length of time the air enters that particular pipe and thus the length of the note. Like the Jacquard cards, these are fastened together to form a 'book'. It is wonderful to think that people still enjoy these colourful machines, but they represent only a side-line in the main story of how the Jacquard card system brought in a technological revolution.

The nineteenth century saw great advances in communication, starting with the electric telegraph, developed by Cooke and Wheatstone, which used electro-magnetism to move needles to indicate letters. The greatest improvement in the system was made by Samuel Morse, who instead of needle indicators, used his famous system of dots and dashes, the Morse code. There were disadvantages to the system in that the time it took to send a message depended on the speed of the operator and errors could easily be made – as I discovered many years ago when taking a Morse course. The answer was to develop a system where the message could be corrected if necessary, stored and then sent on at a later time and the only limiting factor on speed was the system itself. The answer was the punched tape. Émile Baudot developed a system that used five piano-like keys to punch holes that were used as a code. So, for example, for A the operative simply pressed key 1, for B keys 3 and 4, for C 1,3 and 4 and so on. The code, of course,

had to be learned, but was no more difficult to master than the Morse code. The tape was then inserted in the telegraph machine and run through to send the message. Improvements were made by Donald Murray, who still used a version of the Baudot code, but now instead of five keys, used a system very like that of a standard typewriter keyboard to punch the tape. This was the teleprinter and it remained the standard method of communication right up to the modern computer age.

Print remained the main source of providing information to large numbers through newspapers. A German immigrant to America, Ottmar Mergenthaler, developed a revolutionary method of printing. Previously it had relied on type setters, picking individual pieces of type and placing them in the correct order in a case. In the new method, a matrix of type was created. The operator worked at a keyboard to produce punched tape, which was fed to the matrix case, a metal plate with moulds for individual characters. This was placed in the caster, where it could be fed with molten lead. The punched tape determined which mould was to be cast, and the character then appeared in the correct place. It is said that when a visitor first saw the machine in use, he exclaimed in

Richard Dean with the punched card book that controls his fairground organ.

wonder – 'You've just produced a line of type!' And that is how the machine got its name – Linotype. It was first installed at the offices of the New York Tribune in 1886 and soon became the standard method of printing newspapers throughout the world and, like the teleprinter, remained in use until the onset of the computer age, which leads us on to the next major use of the punched tape.

We count using a base of ten, probably because that's how many fingers we have – which makes them useful for calculations. But numbers do not have to be based on 10 – many mathematicians would have preferred a base of 12. The simplest system of all uses 2 as its base. It works just like our familiar system. After 9 we move back to 1 and add a 0. Binary is the same. So, a binary code running up to our number 7 would be - 1, 10, 11, 100, 101, 110, 111. We have already seen a binary system in operation in the Jacquard loom. There the code was for lift, don't lift. It is obvious that it can be adapted to other systems, like the blow, don't blow of the fairground organ. But it could also code for 1 or 0. And that is exactly what was used in the early computers. When in the sixties I worked on X-ray crystallographic data, I had to book a time on the department computer, perhaps getting an hour at infrequent intervals. It was then a case of transferring the data to punched tape. The computer itself was gigantic, occupying the whole of a large room, and yet all it could do was crunch numbers. It had only the fraction of the power of even the cheapest smartphone of today. The idea that it could be used to manipulate words was then unthinkable. But the modern computers still all rely on the same system based on the binary code.

It is, of course, nonsense to think that computer programmers and developers in the twentieth century took their inspiration from a Jacquard card, but it is nevertheless the case that the ideas first worked out two centuries ago were the start of a long period of development. But the punched card, together with the binary code, provided the basis for everything that followed. Perhaps, and indeed probably, someone would have come up with a similar system, but its very first use was in the manufacture of ornate silk fabrics.

We have jumped onwards in time to the modern age, and it is now time to turn the clock back to see what was happening in silk manufacturing in other parts of the world, starting in Britain.

CHAPTER SEVEN

The British Industry

Whenas in silks my Julia goes,
Then, then (methinks) how sweetly flows
The liquefaction of her clothes

Next, when I cast mine eyes and see
That brave vibration each way free;
O how that glittering taketh me!

The seventeenth century English writer Robert Herrick clearly appreciated the special, and obviously rather sexy, qualities of silk. He was far from alone and the British, like other European nations, were enthusiastic buyers of the material. Silk was introduced into Britain in the Medieval period and was at once appropriated for the upper classes. Probably no one else could afford silk, but there were rich merchants who might have thought it appropriate to dress themselves and their families with the luxurious material. A Sumptuary Law of 1363 put a stop to that, specifying exactly who could and could not wear silk. It was totally forbidden for anyone under the rank of knight, and even knights were regulated. A knight worth 500 marks or more could wear what they liked. Those who couldn't meet that standard were told that their wives could not wear silk veils, and the poorest were expressly forbidden from wearing purple silk. As in the Chinese court centuries before, silk was an indicator of rank and importance. There was one exception to the rules on who could wear silk in Elizabethan England; actors were permitted to dress in finery to portray the nobility on stage – but could not wear the same outside the theatre. We know that actors did indeed wear silk on stage. In his biography of Shakespeare, *Will in the World*, Stephen Greenblatt quotes the will of the actor Augustine Phillips in which among other bequests he left one of his apprentices his black taffeta suit. Shakespeare himself managed to purchase a coat of arms for his father, on the grounds that he was a man of independent means who had also held office as the bailiff of Stratford on Avon. Consequently, the playwright and actor could strut his stuff in whatever finery he had.

Silk production did take place in a very small way in England in the Middle Ages, mainly with the weaving of ribbons and small items, but even then it was considered necessary to protect the infant industry by means of a ban on silk imports in the fifteenth century. A similar edict against wearing silk was issued by James III of Scotland in 1472 on the grounds that the country could not afford to import such luxuries. Wearing of silks was again limited to knights worth £100 – though, curiously, silk could be worn by heralds and minstrels. There was also in Scotland opposition to silks from the stern clergy. The General Assembly of the Kirk in 1575 declared, 'We think all kinds of broidering unseemly'. It wanted all the clergy and their wives to dress soberly. 'Their whole habit be of grave colour as black, russet, and grey or sad brown.' At this time, however, it seems there was no actual silk being manufactured in Scotland, but was all imported, mainly through the port of Leith.

The industry in England received a boost in the 1580s when war broke out between Spain and the Netherlands. Protestant Dutch weavers, fearing that the might of Spain might overwhelm their country and enforce conversion to Catholicism, moved to London. They settled in the Spitalfields area, originally Spittle Fields, named after the spittle or hospital of the priory of St. Mary's Spittle, founded in 1197. It was developing as an industrial region outside the city walls, and therefore not subject to the City Laws and restrictions. The weavers soon established a familiar system, based on masters, journeymen and apprentices. The industry became officially recognised in 1628, when silk weavers were incorporated as a City Company. By 1680, the London Weavers' Company had established control over all weaving in the capital and it grew and developed over the next fifty years to the point where it had almost 6,000 members. They were able to lay down strict rules, particularly on apprenticeship. The boy, and they were all males, had to serve a full seven years before qualifying as a journeyman, when he would be allowed to take on work in his own right from one of the masters.

An article on the Spitalfields weavers by Clare Browne details the work of a typical firm of mercers, Francis Rybot and Nicholas Jourdain, who had premises in Raven Row, close to the present Liverpool Street station. Rybot had a trade card describing himself as Weaver and Mercer who 'makes and sells all sorts of rich brocaded silks'. It is unlikely that the partners would have actually woven the cloth themselves, but they would have employed a local pattern drawer to produce an appropriate design and then this would be passed to a master weaver specialising in that sort of cloth – for example he listed damasks and satins among the varieties on offer. They would have sold some of the material from their own shop 'At the sign of The Cat', while some would be sent to locations outside London.

In spite of a modest increase in local production, most silk cloth was imported, largely from France and Italy. James I felt that Britain could compete by developing its own silk worm farms. He ordered a large number of trees for a special Mulberry Garden, very close to the site now occupied by Buckingham Palace. It covered four acres and was tended by the King's Mulberry Men. He also issued an edict that landowners should plant the trees at a rate of six shillings per thousand trees. Unfortunately, the trees he had imported were the black mulberry variety, not the white that the silkworms favoured. It may have been royal ignorance, though it has been suggested that perhaps the French, eager to keep up their trade, deliberately sent him the wrong variety. The king also attempted to persuade farmers in the British colonies of America to abandon what he famously regarded as the pernicious weed, tobacco, in favour of raising silk moths and sending the cocoons back to Britain. The scheme never met with great enthusiasm. In any case, sericulture did not get established in Britain to any meaningful extent, and when an industry did develop, it relied entirely on importing the raw material.

In the early days, all the various processes that preceded weaving – throwing, twisting and doubling – were carried out in London. It is surprising to find that the oldest method of throwing was still being used in the same way in the nineteenth century. The process was described in Lord Shaftesbury's Royal Commission on child labour of 1841:

> For twisting it is necessary to have what are called designated shades which are buildings of at least 30 or 35 yards in length, of two or more rooms, rented separately by one, two or four men having one gate and a boy called a helper … the upper storey is generally occupied by children, young persons or grown women as 'piecers', 'winders' and 'doublers' attending to their reels and bobbins, driven by the exertions of one man … he [the boy] takes first a rod containing four bobbins of silk from the twister who

Silk weavers' houses in Fournier Street, Spitalfields, with the typical workshop garrets at the top.

stands at his gate or wheel, and having fastened the ends, runs to the 'cross' at the extreme end of the room, round which he passes the threads of each bobbin and returns to the 'gate'. He is despatched on a second expedition of the same kind, and returns as before, he then runs up to the cross and detaches the thread and comes to the roller. Supposing the master to make twelve rolls a day, the boy necessarily runs fourteen miles, and this is barefooted.

The process is very basic. Once the boy has attached the threads to the cross, the master turns the wheel, and this imparts the necessary twist.

The weavers from the Netherlands were joined by another, even greater influx of refugee weavers at the end of the seventeenth century. Religious bigotry was once again the cause for bringing skilled workers to Britain, this time from France. In 1598, the Edict of Nantes had allowed a certain amount of freedom to French Protestants to practise their religion. Louis XIV however was a staunch Catholic and in 1685 he revoked the Edict. The French Protestants who supported the reformed form of their religion, as opposed to the Lutherans, were known as Huguenots. Faced with being forced to convert to Catholicism or risk prosecution, many fled to England, skilled weavers amongst them. Almost all they were able to bring with them was specialist knowledge and expertise, but they received a very warm welcome. Using a system called the King's Briefs a subscription was set up to provide funds for their immediate needs. An Order in Council of April 1687 called for a general subscription in the whole country that raised £200,000. That is equivalent to a colossal £30 million at today's value. The sum was large, but so was the problem. It was estimated that around 13,000 Huguenot refugees settled in London. But the knowledge they brought with them was invaluable. They introduced a wide variety of products which had previously only been made in their home cities, Lyon and Tours, such as velvets, brocades and watered silk. Not only did they make these and other cloths themselves, but also taught the techniques to the existing body of Spitalfields weavers. This earned them praise in Stow's Survey of London, a publication which had first appeared at the end of the sixteenth century as a ward by ward survey of the city and which appeared in numerous editions at various intervals. This comment on the Huguenots was part of the entry on Spitalfields:

Here they found quiet and security, and settled themselves in their several trades and occupations, weavers especially. Whereby

An English figured silk waistcoat panel from the early eighteenth century in the Smithsonian Design Museum.

God's blessing surely is not only brought upon the parish by receiving poor strangers, but also a great advantage hath accrued to the whole nation by the rich manufactures of weaving silks and stuffs and camlets, which art they brought along with them. And this benefit also in the neighbourhood, that these strangers may serve for patterns of thrift, honesty, industry and sobriety as well.

One type of cloth that became very popular was figured silk. It was said to have been introduced by three specific weavers – Lauson, Manscot and Monceaux – while the designs were all supplied by the artist, Beaudoin. Another refugee workman brought with him the technology for adding lustre to silk taffeta. This must have been especially galling to the manufacturers of Lyon as black lustrings had been such a major part of their export trade to London that the cloth actually became known as English taffeta. Now the material could be made to the same high standard in Spitalfields. By 1692, the trade had become so well established that a charter was granted to the newly formed Royal Lustring Company. To add insult to injury as far as the French were concerned, the new Company managed to persuade parliament that the local product was now so good that imports from France should be prohibited as they were no longer needed. It is a rather odd argument – if the English material was that brilliant why did it need protecting from foreign competition?

The London silk workers had always struggled to compete with imports from France, and as early as 1696, measures were taken to protect the home industry, by either applying high taxes or even by outright banning of imports. An Act of that year bemoaned the loss of revenue caused by importing silk cloth and claiming it was no longer necessary as it could now be manufactured in England by 'the Royal Lustring Company to as great perfection as in any other country'. But high import duties might have deterred legal trade, but there was still an unsatisfied demand for luxurious French silks and the same Act deplored 'the importation of such foreign silks without paying the duties charged thereon which have been frequently eluded by the subtle practices of evil disposed persons.' Or in plain English – when tariffs are high, smugglers thrive.

To many, smuggling seemed a harmless enough activity, to which the community turned a blind eye, as Kipling wrote in *A Smuggler's Song*:

> Five and twenty ponies
> Trotting through the dark –
> Brandy for the Parson. 'Baccy for the Clerk
> Laces for a lady, letters for a spy.
> Watch the wall my darling while the Gentlemen go by.

But they were by no means all gentlemen, nor indeed gentle men. There seems to have been a distinction between the smugglers of the south west of England and those of the south east. The former seem often to have been fishermen making a bit on the side and otherwise were regarded as respectable members of the community. Those of the south east were often very different, in effect well organised criminal gangs. The south west was not a wealthy area, and tobacco and brandy probably were the most commonly smuggled goods as in the Kipling poem. The market for smuggled silk was in the wealthier area of London and its surroundings, and it was through the south east ports that most of the silk was brought in.

The most infamous of the south east smugglers were the Hawkhurst Gang of Kent. They were ruthless, violent and – although it was difficult to prove against them – were said to threaten death to anyone who informed on them, and almost certainly did carry out that threat. They were brazen, well-armed and defied authority. But in 1747, a young army officer formed a band of vigilantes at a nearby town, calling themselves the Goodhurst Band of Militia, which sounded very respectable, though in fact they had no legal standing at all. That would have not been any great concern to the local authorities who, unable to deal with the gang themselves, were happy to see anyone take them on. A pitched battle was fought in which three smugglers were wounded, and the head of the gang, Thomas Kingsmill, with two companions, captured. Kingsmill was handed over to the authorities, tried, convicted and

Late-eighteenth century silk taffeta dress manufactured in Spitalfields.

hanged. It was the end of the Hawkhurst Gang. It was not the end of smuggling of silk from France, but in spite of that, the home industry continued to grow.

There are still signs of the presence of the weavers in Spitalfields in their distinctive houses, with garrets illuminated by long windows that shed light on the looms. The houses may look grand, but much of the space was taken up for working. A later report described the weavers as usually having two looms, one for himself and one for his wife. As they produced a family, the children were soon set to work, and by the time they were big enough to work a loom, generally at the age of thirteen or fourteen, they too were taught weaving. Eventually, the home might contain up to four looms. With a growing family, the younger children had beds tucked away in corners of the workshop. The houses rarely included any facilities for warping, so this had to be done by specialists, who received the patterns from the master, and arranged the threads in the correct order, and wound them on to the roller for the back of the loom. It was the weaver himself who had to pay for this, not the master. There was also a profitable side-line. Many of the houses had bird traps on the roof, and the songbirds caught were then sold. There are examples of traditional weavers' houses in Fournier Street and Wilkes Street, and their previous occupants would be astonished, and possibly rather disgusted, to discover the prices being asked for their old homes and workshops.

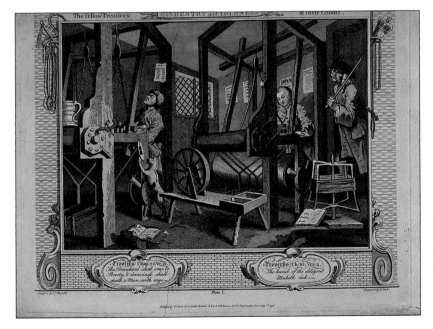

Hogarth's illustration of the idle and good apprentice – one asleep, the other hard at work in Spitalfields, engraved in 1749.

Silk remained an expensive, luxury textile largely because of the high cost of imported yarn. The price was lowered in the early years of the eighteenth century and the story of how it happened is surrounded in mystery and adventure, involving industrial espionage, smuggling and assassination. Just how much of the story is true is a matter of conjecture. It was already known in Britain that the Italians were using machinery to throw and spin silk, but it was said that the details of how the machines worked was a closely guarded secret. The Lombe family were weavers and it was John Lombe who, at the age of 24, was sent by his older brother Thomas to Piedmont to investigate the machinery. He pretended to be an ordinary workman looking for a job and managed to get taken on at one of the spinning mills. While there, he took surreptitious notes and, as soon as he felt he had enough information, made his escape back to England. Once back home, he and his brother set about building a water-powered mill on an island in the River Derwent in Derby and installed the new machinery. The mill was a great success, but the Piedmontese were reportedly furious. They hired a girl who took a position in the Lombe household, where gradually over a period of time she added poison to John Lombe's food. He died in 1722 in mysterious circumstances after a long and painful illness, but everyone in Derby was convinced that he had indeed been poisoned.

How much truth is there in the story? Thomas Lombe, when applying for a patent for the machine, claimed that bringing the machine into the country had cost a great deal both in terms of money and dangers. He repeated the same claims when he later applied for an extension to his patents, this time producing a document in Italian that confirmed a death penalty for anyone who attempted to take the details of the silk machines out of the country. That all seems to tie in with the lurid tale of skulduggery. On the other hand, details of Italian silk machines were available in book form, and a copy of the relevant book was deposited in the Bodleian Library in Oxford. It is of course highly unlikely that Derbyshire weavers regularly used the Bodleian and even if they had seen the book, the description was in Italian and was probably too vague for them to use as a model. Whatever embellishments have been added to the basic story, it remains true that the Lombes did succeed and, although John died young, Thomas became a wealthy man and was later knighted.

William Hutton wrote about the mill in his *History of Derby* published in 1785. He described the mill as containing three engines:

the first to wind, the second to twist and the third to double. In the following short extract, he is describing the winding process:

> The threads are continually breaking; and to tye them is principally the business of children whose fingers are nimble. The machine continually turns the round bobbin or small block of wood, which draws the thread from the slip (skein) ... one person commands from twenty to sixty threads.

Hutton had himself been one of those children, whose nimble fingers were employed, and he did not enjoy the experience:

> All the visitors who have travelled to Derby for half a century, from Gregory to Gough, give us a description of the silk-mill. But it is doubtful whether an adequate idea can be formed of that wonderful machine when described by an author who does not understand it himself. Some have earnestly wished to see this singular piece of mechanism, but I have sincerely wished I never had seen it. I have lamented that while almost every man in the world was born *out* of Derby it should be my unhappy lot to be born *in*. To this curious, but wretched

Derby silk mill, with the small original Crotchett silk mill to the right.

place, I was bound apprentice for seven years, which I always considered the most unhappy of my life ... My parents, through mere necessity, put me to labour before Nature had made me able. Low as the engines were, I was too short to reach them. To remedy this defect, a pair of high pattens were fabricated, and lashed to my feet which I dragged after me till time lengthened my stature. The confinement and the labour were no burden; but the severity was intolerable, the marks of which I yet carry and shall carry to my grave.

Hutton gave only perfunctory details of the workings of the mill. The building was five storeys high, the top three storeys being used for winding and the two lower floors for throwing and doubling. Power was supplied by an imposing water wheel, 23ft in diameter and 6ft wide. The machines themselves were circular, between 12 and 15ft in diameter and 19ft 8in high. The twist mill consisted of four rounds of spindles, mounted one above the other. Power from the wheel was transmitted through gearing to a vertical axis that ran up through the different floors. The inner framework was turned by the wheel; the outer frame was stationary. Throwing involved unwinding the silk from one rotating bobbin and passing it through a flyer to give twist and winding on to a second set of bobbins. The actual mechanism for getting all the parts to move in the correct way was complex and distinctly clumsy. Once the Lombe patent expired, several manufacturers began improving on the original design.

The Derby silk mill is often referred to as Britain's first textile factory, but in fact a mill had already been built on the Derwent in Derby in 1702 for silk throwing. It was three storeys high and contained Dutch doubling machines. It was the brainchild of a barrister 'Thomas Crotchett' and the actual job of constructing the mill was entrusted to the engineer George Sorocold. It is generally considered not to have been very efficient. Commentators noted that the mechanism was quite crude, nevertheless when Lombe came to build his mill, he chose the site next to the Crotchett mill, which he incorporated into the new system – and although the old machinery was said to be less perfect it remained in use until 1802. And Lombe must have been sufficiently impressed to employ Sorocold as the engineer for his own enterprise. The modest Crotchett mill can be seen rather overwhelmed by the grandeur of the Lombe mill in the illustration (p 103). It seems that Crotchett

Derby silk mill photographed before it was severely damaged by fire in 1910.

deserves more credit than he is usually given – and might well stake a claim to having beaten Lombe to the honour of establishing the first textile mill in Britain. The production of cloth, however, still remained up to individual weavers, such as those of Spitalfields.

Early in the eighteenth century, the Spitalfields weavers had tried to get French imports banned to protect their trade, but then a new rival appeared on the scene. The British originally went to the Far East in the hope of joining the highly lucrative trade in exotic spices but discovered that the Dutch had got there first and more or less monopolised the business. Unable to get a foothold in the Spice Islands, they went instead to India. They then looked around for items that might be bought and shipped to Britain to make a profit. They found that the Indians had perfected a method of creating colourful cotton cloths, by adding a mordant to the cloth that could hold a dye. They then created patterns that could be placed on the cloth, so that the exposed sections could take the dye. Later, a technique was developed by printing the cloth using carved wooden blocks. The block cutters didn't even need to own workshops. They simply turned up with blocks of wood and cutting tools at wherever the cloth was being made, and carved whatever patterns were required. Craftsmen still do this today, and it is amazing to see just how quickly a pattern can be carved by eye alone. In the process I was watching, the pattern being printed was a very popular one 'The Tree of Life'. The colourful, patterned cloth made by selective dyeing was known as 'chint', later Anglicized to 'chintz'. And because much of the cloth was sent out from the port of Calicut, many of the cloths were given the name calico, though with several variations in spelling.

At first, the new materials were used for quilts and bedspreads, but by the beginning of the eighteenth century, the advantages of a light, colourful and – in comparison with silk – affordable material brought about a major change. The Indian materials started to be used for dresses and became immensely fashionable to the considerable dismay of the silk weavers. They found a champion in Daniel Defoe, now mainly known as the author of *Robinson Crusoe* but in his day a highly respected political commentator. In 1719, he wrote a number of pamphlets lambasting the taste for cotton. The following extract is typical:

> The general fantasies of the people running upon East India goods to that degree that the chintz and painted calicoes

In the eighteenth century, new materials arrived in Britain to challenge silk; a cotton dress in Indian Chintz on display in the Fashion Museum, Antwerp.

which before were only made use of for carpets, quilts, &c, and to clothe children and ordinary people, became now the dress of our ladies, and such is the power of a mode as we saw our persons of quality dressed in Indian carpets, which but a few years before their chambermaids would have thought too ordinary for them.

There were even popular broad sheet ballads, decrying the new fashions, such as one called the *Ballad of Spitalfields* or the *Weavers Complaint against the Calicoe Madams*. It is rather long, but a couple of verses give the flavour. It starts with a verse about the good old days, then continues:

> But now we bring Home
> The Froth and the Scum
> To Dress up the Trope like a gay-Dame
> And Ev'ry She Clown
> Gets a Pye-spotted Gown
> And sets up for a Calicoe Madam
> O! Tawdery Calicoe Madam.
>
> Were there ever such Fools
> Who despising the Rules.
> For the common Improvement of Nations,
> Tye up the Poor's Hands
> And search foreign lands,
> For the Magpie Ridiculous Fashions
> For the Magpie Ridiculous Fashions.

Where Defoe's sarcastic comments and ballads had little effect, the Spitalfields weavers took matters into their own hands in 1719. On 13 June of that year, a crowd estimated at some 4,000 silk weavers took to the streets and attacked women wearing calico, spattering their clothes with ink or, more dangerously, nitric acid to rot the cloth. The Mayor of London called in the military to help quell the riot and the Horse Grenadiers managed to capture two men and marched them off to the Marshalsea Prison. But as soon as they had gone, the riots broke out again. The troops returned and more arrests were made. A body of weavers then attempted to release their comrades. At first, the soldiers repelled them by firing blank cartridges into the crowd, and when that looked to be ineffective, one of the Guards fired ball shot. Three weavers were wounded, and the rest dispersed. Over the next couple of days, six weavers were tried and sent to Newgate Prison for felony. At least one lady went into print to condemn 'a gang of audacious rogues to come and fall on us in the streets, and tear the clothes off our backs, insult and chase us, and tell us we shall not wear what they do not weave; is this to be allowed in a Nation of Liberty.'

In fact, this was something of a false alarm as the silk industry was actually prospering and by 1721 was officially described as being 'one of the most considerable branches of manufactures of the kingdom'. And the government gave positive help to the industry by helping to fund part of the duty that had to be paid when importing the raw material. They also imposed high duties on imported silk cloth and goods. This, however, did not prevent the materials arriving in Britain illegally, and silk smuggling became a highly lucrative business. But that alone did not satisfy the weavers, who found French silks outselling their own wares, while at the same time they were suffering from increasing poverty. There was a specific problem facing the weavers. A lot of the work involved creating elaborate patterns, using draw looms. Setting up such a loom could take as much as three weeks, during which time they were paying an idle draw boy and not earning any money. To make matters worse, the elaborate cloths were only produced in short lengths, typically just enough to make four gowns. Then as now, a lady who had paid a great deal of money for an expensive and elaborate cloth for her new dress did not take kindly to seeing dozens of other ladies wearing the same pattern. By the 1760s, with wages low and smuggling rampant, the trade was in a desperate state, with over 7,000 looms idle. The weavers got together that year and presented the owners with a Book of Prices, setting out what they felt were fair returns for different types of material. As the prices were somewhat higher than the masters were paying at the time, the Book was rejected. It marked the start of a period of prolonged violence that grew worse over the next few years.

By 1763, with no relief in sight and no rise in wages, the weavers began attacking masters who were considered particularly harsh. One such event was described in *The Gentleman's Magazine* of November 1763. The men 'in riotous manner broke into the house of one of their masters, destroyed his looms, and cut a great quantity of silk to pieces, after which they placed an effigy in a cart, with a halter about his neck, an executioner at one side, and a coffin on the other, and after drawing it through the streets they hanged it on a gibbet, then burnt it to ashes.'

By the beginning of January 1764, the trade depression had deepened and weavers petitioned parliament to impose a double tax on imported silk. That idea was rejected, but the tax on silk thread brought in for the weavers was reduced and certain silk imports – stockings, ribbons and gloves – were banned. A fund was set up to relieve the worst of the weavers' poverty and mercers promised to reduce their stock of imported silks. None of this made a real difference apart from creating a temporary lull in the violence, and soon the demand to stop imports was renewed. It was rejected once again in May 1765, and among the leaders opposing any change in the law was the Duke of Bedford. He had his own interest to look after as he had connections with the East India Company and was enjoying a handsome income from importing Indian cotton. The crowds who had gathered outside parliament to harangue the Lords were quickly dispersed by the military, but the angry mob set off for Bloomsbury and the Duke of Bedford's house. Seeing exactly what was likely to happen, the Duke called in the military, and troops arrived on horseback just in time to prevent the weavers storming the house.

The authorities were by now seriously alarmed by the growing anger in Spitalfields and the surrounding weaving districts, and had troops permanently stationed there, like an occupying army. It did little to improve the air of desperation among the suffering families. Ever more draconian measures were introduced to support the masters, reaching a deadly climax in 1765, when a law was passed declaring that breaking into a house to cut up silk or damage looms was a felony punishable by death. In response, secret societies were set up. They were similar to those of the earlier Luddites who had tried to get justice by threatening to break up the machines used for knitting stockings in Nottinghamshire unless the masters agreed to obey the law of the land and stop employing apprentices instead of journeymen to do the work. The weavers attempted to ensure that no weavers worked for lower rates and demanded subscriptions from the masters. They used the threat of machine breaking and cloth cutting to try and force through their demands.

Attempts to prosecute the militant weavers generally came to nothing, largely because the fear of reprisals prevented witnesses appearing in court. One manufacturer, who was vehement in his opposition to the whole idea of raising wages, was Lewis Chauvet who owned a factory in Spitalfields. He offered a reward of £500 to anyone prepared to give evidence against the weavers. This encouraged one master weaver and his wife to come forward and identify John Villers and John Doyle as ringleaders of the cutters. They were arrested, tried and inevitably found guilty and sentenced to death. Public executions were normally held at Tyburn, but this time the authorities decided there would be far more impact if the hanging took place in Bethnal Green in the heart of the silk weaving region. The event caused outrage, and the unfortunate man given the job of erecting the gibbet was stoned and abused by the crowd. On the day of execution, the actual hanging was brought forward secretly for fear of the crowd that was threatening to develop. In those brutal days, the bodies were left hanging for hours before their relatives could claim them.

Now another small master 'Daniel Clarke' came forward with two names. His house had been broken into some weeks before and when questioned at the time had stated quite categorically that he had no idea who the intruders were. Now he named them as John William Eastman and William Harfield. Whether this sudden return of memory was due to a brave decision to tell the truth and risk the wrath of the mob or the Chauvet pieces of silver was never clear, though most of the residents of Spitalfields had no doubts on the subject. The two accused were duly hanged – this time at Tyburn; the authorities had at least learned one lesson. If Clarke had testified for money, he did not live long to enjoy it. He was spotted in the street and pursued by a mob, mainly of women and children, who caught him, threw him into a flooded gravel pit and pelted him with stones. He emerged, but promptly collapsed and died. Once again, the authorities acted swiftly. Quite how they decided who out of that great crowd should be charged is a mystery, but two men were selected: Henry Stroud and Eastman's brother-in-law, Robert Campbell. They were charged with murder and hanged. They were desperate times and the brutal action of the authorities did little to help calm the situation.

Something like normality was restored with the passing of the first Spitalfields Act in 1773, which set the prices for the different categories of silk by an agreement between journeymen and masters. A series of similar Acts followed, which stabilised the relationship between masters and men, but worked against the long-term interests of the industry. If the price was fixed for a certain class of weaving, then there was no incentive for the master to modernise his methods, for any changes he made would have no effect on the price. But the textile world in other parts of Britain was changing rapidly, and the Spitalfields Acts only applied locally.

One of the innovations that speeded up work on the loom was the invention of the flying shuttle by John Kay of Bury in 1733. Previously, the shuttle had been passed from one side of the loom to the other by hand which, in the case of broadcloth, required two weavers. In the new technology, the hands of the weavers were replaced by two leather drivers, or pickers on a metal rod. The shuttle was put on wheels and it shot from one side of the loom to the other. All the weaver had to do was jerk a string attached to the pickers. This obviously increased efficiency, but as time went on, the supply of thread was not keeping pace with the increased speed of weaving. This was particularly true of the burgeoning cotton industry. The answer was to take the early production stages of carding and spinning away from the home and into the factory. The first successful water powered cotton mill was built by Richard Arkwright at Cromford in Derbyshire in 1771. In spite of fierce opposition from the domestic spinners of Lancashire, who burned down the first Arkwright mill to be built in their area, the mills proliferated, and the days of cottage industry spinning and carding were over. New machines, such as the spinning jenny, steadily increased efficiency. By the end of the century, water-power was being replaced by steam-power in the textile mills of the north. The other major change – the introduction of the power loom – has already been described.

These technological changes did not affect the silk weavers of Spitalfields directly. The power looms were too violent in their action for the delicate silk threads. But in the long term, the developments in the north were to make a huge difference. The silk weavers were not producing for a mass market. Fashions were changing in Georgian England, where a new, loose neo-classical look was becoming dominant. Heavy brocades and velvets were out and light, colourful fabrics were in. This was a fashion that the cotton industry was able to supply at a far lower cost than the handloom weavers of London. They could have continued supplying the most exclusive fabrics, but for two pieces of legislation that completely changed the economic climate. In 1824, under Free Trade legislation, the Spitalfields Acts were repealed and price fixing was ended. The following year the ban on imported French silks was lifted, and at once the market was flooded with attractive new, reasonably produced materials. It was a watershed that marked the beginning of the end for silk weaving in Spitalfields. But it did not mark the end of the silk industry in the country as a whole. Where the Spitalfields Acts did not apply, there was no brake on innovation and change.

CHAPTER EIGHT

Silk Outside London

There were many reasons why masters might want to leave London, apart from the various riots that had darkened the scene. For some it was simply a chance to extend their business on their own terms, without the restrictions imposed by the Spitalfields Acts. Suffolk had been an important area for woollens since medieval times, but the introduction of water-powered machinery gave the north of England with its fast-flowing streams and rivers an overwhelming advantage. By the end of the eighteenth century, the industry was in terminal decline, but it did have a large population of skilled weavers. Sudbury was the town chosen for major developments; one advantage it had was that it lay at the head of the Stour Navigation, which made it ideal for importing raw material and exporting finished products. The Vanner brothers, of Huguenot stock, moved here in the late eighteenth century and their descendants are still here today. They began using Jacquard looms, but by 1900 they had power looms installed in a new factory but still in Sudbury, where they continue to manufacture silk and have their own dyeing and cloth finishing departments. They were to be followed by other London weavers and by 1844 there were approximately 600 looms in the town. Others followed.

Benjamin Walters was a weaver in Paternoster Row, London, in 1720 and his son Joseph followed him in the trade. Joseph's son – Joseph Walters II – was also to become a weaver but, rather than teach the boy himself, his father sent him as an apprentice to John Dubois. It seems that, even in the early eighteenth century, the Huguenots still had a reputation as being the finest craftsmen in the region. Joseph and his brother George set up business and home in Wilkes Street, Spitalfields. Eventually, the family business grew too big for the house in Wilkes Street, and they established what might well have been the first silk weaving factory in London, though still using hand looms. Over the years, they moved further and further out of London and at Kettering they established a factory that was one of the pioneers in using power looms. By 1860, they had established a factory in Sudbury and the family business is still there today as Stephen Walters.

Their reputation was so good that they received a number of high prestige commissions, including weaving the material for both Princess Anne and Princess Diana's wedding dresses. They clearly benefitted from the experience that Joseph II gained from his Huguenot connection, though his old teacher would no doubt be astonished if he visited the modern factory to see the high-speed rapier looms controlled by computers.

Gwen Curtis working at Walters factory on a fifty year old loom, weaving a silk lining for the coronation robe for Queen Elizabeth II.

A modern rapier, shuttleless loom at the Walters silk factory.

Sudbury remains the major centre for silk weaving in Britain and there are still memories of the former handloom days in streets of old weavers' cottages that survive in the town, easily recognised by the large windows that mark the position of workshops. A row in Cross Street, for example, had living quarters on the ground floor, well lit workshops on the floor above, and bedrooms above that. It was not the only place weaving silk in the early eighteenth century, and one notable mill in Hampshire went through several different owners, including for a short time, Stephen Walters. The Hayter family began building a water-powered mill at Whitchurch in Hampshire in 1813 on land owned by the Dean and Chapter of Winchester Cathedral. Unfortunately, the family went bankrupt in 1817 and the mill was sold to a silk merchant, William Maddick. He set about making improvements, adding a middle floor to the mill and creating the mill pond. The yarn was prepared in the main mill building, which was flanked by single-storey weaving sheds. It had a somewhat chequered history, changing hands several times. In 1845, it was taken over by the Chappell family but when Adelaide Chappell was widowed, she found it difficult to keep the business going. She sold off the northern weaving shed, which was converted into four cottages. By 1886, however, she was no longer able to cope, and once again the mill came on the market. This time it was bought by a local draper for his son, James Hyde. This marked the start of a long period of successful work, mainly weaving coloured silk linings for Burberry raincoats.

The new owners made improvements, including installing a new waterwheel with the latest developments, including a centrifugal governor that controlled the flow of water to the wheel. This is a device usually seen on steam engines. A pair of heavy metal balls are attached to a central spindle – as the flow of water increases and the wheel speeds up, so too does the spindle, so that the balls are forced further apart by centrifugal force. This action is geared to a system that raises and lowers boards between the mill stream and the wheel. The mill continued to struggle financially, and in 1956 Stephen Walters & Son stepped in to try and keep the historic site going. It was to have one other owner before it was taken over in 1985 in a fairly derelict condition by Hampshire Building Preservation Trust who restored it as a working industrial museum.

The eighteenth century silk mill at Whitchurch, Hampshire.

The main building is a reminder that the period we now refer to in Britain as the Industrial Revolution was also the Georgian age, which was notable for the elegant, classical simplicity of its architecture. Whitchurch Mill could easily be mistaken for a rather grand country house were it not for the little clock tower on the roof. The clock itself was installed to celebrate the victory at Waterloo and has been ticking away merrily ever since. Inside the main building, the ground floor is largely taken up with conventional power looms. Unfortunately, the low ceilings have never made it impossible to install the tall Jacquard mechanism. The winder on the upper floor is still geared in to the water wheel, and it is here that warping takes place. It is the last working silk mill in Britain that still uses any form of water-power in its processes and today produces specialist, high quality silk cloth. It is a reminder, too, that silk weaving has never had an easy passage in this country, as the many different owners testify. It is also, perhaps, somewhat surprising to find a thriving silk mill in this area. But the silk industry was never limited to one area. Even in the heart of the West of England, where the Gloucestershire mills were famous for producing woollen cloth, many silk mills thrived for a time. Blockley is now thought of as a quaint Cotswold village, yet silk throwing mills existed here as early as the start of the eighteenth century. The trade only died away completely in the 1880s, but for a time it was an important centre for silk throwing, mostly supplying yarn to the ribbon weavers of Coventry. Many other Gloucestershire mills were used for silk throwing for a time, mostly being converted from older woollen mills. In the latter part of the nineteenth century it was estimated that there were about 1,000 workers employed in the industry in the five valleys centred on Stroud. The other important centre in the county was Tewkesbury, where they specialised in manufacturing silk stockings. Many counties which we no longer associate with the industry had important centres for silk manufacture, several of which had their own specialities.

Coventry was one of the biggest customers for Gloucestershire throwing mills, where the silk ribbon industry was established early in the eighteenth century. It followed the usual pattern of masters sending the raw material to outworkers with their own looms. There are few reminders of the industry today in the city, but in its heyday, it was reckoned that almost half the population of Coventry were involved in the trade. I was actually totally unaware of the trade when I came to Coventry by canal in the 1970s, but I do remember being surprised to see a row of cottages on the canal side as we approached the city that had the unmistakable large windows that indicated hand working had once gone on inside.

Ribbon weaving seems to have first arrived, as did so many other branches of the industry, with Huguenot refugees. That it thrived and was a major employer can be gauged by the story of just one manufacturer, Thomas Bird, who died in 1756 and whose obituary stated that he daily employed over 2,000 weavers. This seems an extraordinarily large number, but at this time all the ribbons were hand woven on narrow looms, only able to weave a single ribbon. This was very delicate work, with the shuttle simply being passed using the fingers and it was possible to add decorative details, such as beading. When wider looms were introduced, capable of weaving several ribbons at once, this was no longer possible, so the hand-woven ribbons from the narrow looms were always special and enabled the craft to continue well into the machine age. The weavers at one time were paid one third of the price received when the goods were sold from the master's warehouse.

The Cash family were prominent Quakers, who took an unusually benevolent interest in their workers' welfare. Joseph Cash and sons Josiah and John began making ribbons in 1846, when they had offices and a warehouse in Hertford Street with a factory at West Orchard – a site now occupied by a shopping centre. They provided allotments for their workers and established a nursery school for the families in the grounds of their home. They were well aware that the days of the handloom were drawing to a close, but rather than simply build a weaving mill and hiring a workforce, they set up a system that was a sort of half-way house between home weaving and a factory. They built Cash's Top Shops in 1857. These consisted of two rows of conventional two-storey cottages, built to a high standard and each one having its own little garden. But on the third floor was the loom workshop, with immense windows. Each weaver had his own access to the workshop from his home, and here the Cashes installed Jacquard looms, powered by a steam engine in the courtyard and with line shafting and belts driving the looms. The workers also had a number of benefits, including a canteen, sickness benefits and an annual trip to the seaside, paid for by the company. Things went well at first, but in 1860, the Free Trade Bill became law, and England was flooded with cheap French ribbons. It was the death knell for ribbon weaving in Coventry, but Cash's adapted. Instead of ribbons they started a profitable

Ribbon loom manufactured by T. Wilkinson of Coventry circa. 1910 with Jacquard attachment that weaves four ribbons simultaneously, now in the Manchester Museum of Science and Industry.

business weaving name tags and labels. All over Britain in the first part of the twentieth century, mothers would be taking strips of name tags, cutting them into sections and sewing them into school uniforms. The family continued with the business right up to 1976. The Top Shops are still there, right alongside the Coventry Canal but no longer in use.

The crash of the 1860s saw mass unemployment among weavers and it has been estimated that some 9,000 people left the city in just two years, many of them emigrating. One man who, like the Cash family, found a solution to the problem by starting in a new line of business was Thomas Stevens. He was involved, like many others, in weaving plain and fancy ribbons and had premises in Queen Street, but he was also something of an innovator. He began using the Jacquards to weave coloured silk pictures. He could use the ribbon looms for the work – with the pattern repeating. He then used the designs not to create ribbons but bookmarks. One special bookmark that he created to mark the opening of the Coventry Market Hall

Cash's Top Shops in Coventry; the workers lived in the terraced houses, with the workshops above them on the top floor.

A silk bookmark by T. Stevens of Coventry, 1871.

in 1867 was 13 inches long and required a total of 5,500 Jacquard cards to complete the design. By 1862, he was selling a range of bookmarks, from quite simple ones costing just sixpence each to large elaborate ones for church Bibles costing fifteen shillings. He was always on the lookout for new openings and managed to obtain a contract from the Admiralty for sailors' hat ribbons with the name of the ship woven in gold. The business kept expanding and new premises were built in West Orchard and when that proved inadequate, a third factory was established in Cox Street. At the same time, the pictorial ware was given a new trade name – Stevengraph – and was soon winning medals at trade fairs around the world. The works continued being run by the family but the Cox Street factory was bombed into oblivion, like so much else in Coventry, in the air raids of the Second World War.

Another town that began with a specialist trade was Macclesfield, which was known for manufacturing ornate buttons as early as the middle of the seventeenth century. Silk buttons in particular became a must have for the fashionable ladies and gentlemen of the time. They were embroidered by hand on wooden moulds. The work was almost entirely done by women and children and, in 1698, the Corporation issued an instruction that 'poor children and the poor' should be taught button making. Many of the buttons were sold wholesale and the rest were sold around the country by chapmen or pedlars. Many of them came from the settlement of Flash, which had been built up by individuals on the wasteland and led to them being known as 'Flashmen'. The cost of imported silk from countries such as Turkey was more than balanced by the return export of woollens. But hand-made silk buttons were expensive, and cheaper versions that could be made to look quite gaudy found a ready market. The government saw the import of silk falling and with it the valuable exports, so they issued a law in 1709 forbidding 'the making or selling Buttons made of Cloth Serge Drugget or other Stuffs'. Anyone found doing so was fined five pounds for every dozen buttons. Enforcing the Act proved difficult and it was, in any case, self-defeating at least according to Jon Aitken in his book *A Description of the Country from Thirty to Forty Miles round Manchester* (1795). 'Hired informers were engaged in London and the country – an odious and very uncommercial mode of enforcing a manufacture! The result of which was to promote the use of metal and horn buttons.'

It was inevitable that, following the success of the Derby mill, a town with such a large number of people working with silk would

An eighteenth century English silk button on a wooden mould.

want to follow Lombe's example. The first small mill was built by Charles Roe at Park Green in the 1740s and was soon followed by others. Financing this new industry was not a problem for Roe, who had developed a new interest in copper mining and smelting, which was to turn more profitable than he could ever have imagined. His agent made a remarkable discovery that a modest hill on Anglesey called rather too grandly Parys Mountain was in fact one of the richest sources of copper ore ever found in Britain. Its exploitation was so successful that it brought the traditional copper mines of Cornwall and Devon close to bankruptcy for a time. For a while, Macclesfield was one of the leading manufacturers of silk in the country, and when Sir Frank Warner wrote his history of the silk industry in 1921, it was still thriving. The mills have now all closed, but the town is still home to two very fine museums to the industry, demonstrating both the machinery and the wares.

There were areas of silk production on various scales throughout much of Britain, but one more place deserves a special mention as it has given its name to an enduringly popular design: Paisley. The manufacture was started in about 1760 by Humphrey Fulton. He had begun his working life as a packman, a type of travelling salesman. He then began to manufacture linen before turning to silk gauzes in imitation of the work he had seen in Spitalfields in his packman days. The business was a success and he was soon said to have between 400 and 600 looms working in the town. His success soon brought imitators, including companies from London, attracted by the low wages being paid in Scotland. Later the manufacturers turned to muslin, which attracted the attention of Daniel Defoe as he made his great Tour through the Whole Island of Great Britain between 1724 and 1726:

> Here is a manufacture of muslins, and perhaps the only manufacture of its kind in Britain, if not in Europe, and they make them so good and so fine, that great quantities of them are sent into England, and sold there at a good price; they are generally strip'd and are very much used for aprons by the ladies, and sometimes in head-clothes by the English women of a meaner sort, and many of them are sent to the English plantations.

By 1781, there were reported to be 4,800 silk looms at work. As with other regions, Paisley silk weavers were badly hit by the introduction of factories producing cheap cotton yarn, which inevitably meant cheaper cloth. Having made fine muslins, the weavers began to think of making shawls with oriental patterns. One particular pattern, based on ornate teardrop shapes, had originated in Persia in the third century. The pattern was supposed to represent a cypress tree, a Zoroastrian symbol for eternal life. The design was used widely in Asia and the Middle East. One variety was made in Kashmir from the fine hair of local goats and an example turned up in France during the reign of Louis XIV, where Kashmir became 'cachemire' and later in Britain, cashmere. Guilllaume Louis Ternaux decided that he would make these shawls and a party was sent to Kashmir to buy a herd of goats. Of the 1,500 animals that started the journey, only 256 made it alive to France, but that proved enough to make a start. Soon, shawls were being made in a variety of materials, including silk. The fashion spread across the Channel, and they began making shawls in Paisley. It proved a highly lucrative trade and by 1834 was calculated to be worth a million pounds. The weavers stuck to

A nineteenth century paisley shawl now in the Auckland Museum, having been brought to New Zealand by the donor's grandmother.

the original design and it became so associated with the town that it soon became known simply as paisley – as it still is. But trade too often goes down as rapidly as it goes up. In 1838 an anonymous witness to a Parliamentary Enquiry of 1838 gave his views of the weavers' plight in verse.

> Hard is your fortune, nurslings of the loom,
> Cradled in sorrow, reared in joyless toil;
> Stumbling and lost in dull commercial gloom,
> Uncheered by hope, your anguish to beguile.

The silk industry as a whole, however, received a major boost, when a new method was found for using the raw material.

CHAPTER NINE

Waste Silk

The term 'waste silk' is somewhat misleading, suggesting a material that has no value at all. Basically, it refers to any silk that isn't suitable for reeling. This can be from a number of different reasons. The moth may already have started emerging from the cocoon. The thread that makes up the cocoon is uneven, with the outer part too thick and the inner part too thin. The cocoon may simply have been damaged or the raw silk might have needed re-reeling, during which process breakages had occurred – the latter was known in the trade as 'gum-waste' because the gummy substance that holds everything together in the cocoon has not been removed. As mentioned in Chapter One, even in the earliest days of silk manufacture, a use was found for waste silk for a filling for padded garments.

There must have been an abundance of waste silk from the earliest days of manufacturing in China, just as there was in later years when production was established in Europe. There is, however, very little evidence to show how it was used. There are references to its use as stuffing, when it was imported into Britain, as 'soldiers' bedding' to be spun in mills. One of the earliest references comes from Jean-Baptiste du Halde, *The General History of China* (1736), 'As the Chinese are very skilful in counterfeiting, they make a false sort of Kientcheou with the waste of the Tehi-Kiang silk, which without due inspection, might easily be taken for the right.' As du Halde had never himself visited China, but based his book on reports sent back by Jesuit missionaries, the claim of counterfeiting might not be taken too seriously. Later references refer to carded silk being used to make 'durable dresses for the peasantry'. Evidence of the spinning of short-fibred silk in Asia can be traced back for centuries. In India there was a long tradition of manufacturing Eri silk. This comes not from the *Bombyx Mori* but from *Samia Ricini*, a moth whose caterpillars feed on the leaves of the castor plant. Because the silk produced has short, quite coarse fibres it had to be carded and spun, like cotton – the system that would need to be applied to work waste silk. A. Yusuf Ali in a monograph of 1900 described the manufacture of Eri silk in detail, and then went on:

> In the case of the mulberry feeding silkworm, after the glossy portion has been reeled off there is a small quantity of fluffy fibre which cannot be reeled and is called waste silk or *chashm*. This is mixed with some pea flour and boiled, while still moist and warm, thus dissolving any mucilaginous matter that there may be in it, and rendering the substance soft and pliable. After being dried this *chashm* of bombycide silk is spun and twisted in the same way as Eli silk.

As we know that Eri silk has been made for centuries, it seems reasonable to assume that as the technology was available, carding and spinning waste silk has a similarly long history in Asia. We just don't know how long.

Eri silk moths from an Indian silk farm.

At first, as far as Europeans were concerned, the waste silk was considered to have only small value. It was imported as 'nubs'

or 'knubbs', and an official document of 1593 shows that long raw silk was roughly ten times as valuable as nubs. Because the silk cannot be reeled it has to be carded and spun, just as other materials such as wool and cotton are treated. Carding gets its name from the earliest form in which it appeared. This used a pair of boards studded with wire, which were held in the hand, and the fibres were laid across one, while the other was pulled across. This disentangled and straightened the fibres. In the eighteenth century, hand cards were replaced by mechanical cards, using a wire studded drum, powered at first by water and later by steam. The good quality short fibres treated in this way are known as noil silk. In France and Piedmont, raw silk was also treated by carding. Silk that was slightly inferior, perhaps rather weak or coarse, was carded and spun to create what were called Floretta, described by Ephraim Chambers in the *Cyclopedia of the Arts and Sciences* (1728) as 'a tolerable silk'. Chambers then goes on to describe the treatment of silk from damaged cocoons.

> As to the balls, after opening them with scissors and taking out the insects (which are of some use for the feeding of poultry), they are steeped three or four days in troughs, the water whereof is changed every day to prevent their stinking. When they are well softened by this scouring and cleared of that gummy matter, the worms had lined the inside with, and which renders it impermeable to water, they boil them half an hour in a ley of ashes, very clear and well strained; and after washing them out in the river and drying them in the sun they card and spin them on the wheel, &c, and thus make another kind of Floretta, somewhat inferior to the former.

'Floretta' is just one version of the French 'fleuret' and the English 'floret', but it is the French version that came into general use when referring to silk. The spoiled cocoons were boiled, dried and beaten, and in the early days, the cocoons were then set onto a distaff, broken open and fibres pulled out to arm's length at each side. The fibres were then carded and spun. Over the years, the English version of the word fleuret became the rather less romantic floss. The yarn that was produced was only rarely used for making cloth, but was generally sold on bobbins, and was ideal for use in embroidery. These yarns were being made in France as early as the sixteenth century.

The interest shown in utilising waste silk is hardly surprising, since between broken cocoons and damage during reeling and doubling, there was in any processing generally more waste than usable fine silk. Inventors soon began applying their ingenuity to finding new and improved ways of using this material. One of the earliest applications for a patent was made by Edmond Blood of London in 1671. His description of his invention was notably short of detail:

> A NEW manufacture, being a Rich Silk Shagg commodious for Garments, made of a Silk Wast, hitherto of little or no use, and shagged by Tezell or Rowing Cards, like an English Bayes, Rowed Fustians or Dimatyes, a sort of Manufacture never before knowne or made in this our Kingdome.

Apart from the archaic spellings, it is fairly clear what he was making, even if it is far less obvious just how he was doing so. Teasel heads were regularly used in the woollen industry to raise the nap of the cloth, either in the form of hand held cards or in teasel gig mills. In the latter, the plant heads were set in batons fixed to the rim of a rotating drum, over which the cloth was passed. A rare survivor of this type of machine, powered by a water wheel, can be seen at Dunkirk Mill, Nailsworth, and is regularly demonstrated to the public. 'Rowing' refers to roving cards, which do the same job as the teasels. 'Shagg' is what is now known as shag, a material with a rough surface – most people come across the word in shag pile carpets. 'Bayes' is baize. In a further note, Blood indicated that his silk shag could either be used on its own or mixed with linen. He does not appear to have placed a very high estimate on the value of his invention, as all he was asking for its use was an annual rent of six shillings and eight pence, slightly over a hundred pounds at today's prices.

The eighteenth century saw the appearance of more patents for treating waste, among which was one by Dr Edmund Cartwright, famous for his power loom. On this occasion, however, his machine for combing seems never to have actually gone into production. Even in the heart of the cotton industry of Lancashire, there was one manufacturer, Thomas Wood of Holcombe, who patented a machine for carding and roving silk – though it too never left the page to turn into physical reality. So, throughout a long period, lasting right up to the end of the eighteenth century, waste silk remained the poor relation.

One reason why waste silk did not become a really useful material was the method of manufacture. The process began with passing the waste through a breaker to disentangle the worst of the knotty connections, dressing it and then cutting it into lengths of about two inches. As one of the great virtues of silk is the length of the fibre, it seems perverse to cut it up, but one can see why. The rest of the processing was similar to that for other fibres, such as flax and cotton. The material was first scutched – a process used for flax – which involved using a wooden device called a knife, which removed any loose, unwanted material from the fibres. It was then carded and prepared for spinning. At the beginning of the nineteenth century, most spinning used mules. These are ingenious devices, originally developed for the cotton industry. To put it briefly, the mule consisted of a fixed section, with the unspun, but loosely wound, cotton on a row of bobbins. From these, the thread was taken to spindles, mounted on a wheeled carriage. The process starts with the carriage moving away from the main frame, drawing out the cotton, and then, at the end of the run, the spindles turn to impart twist, after which the carriage returns, and the twisted yarn is wound onto the spindles, ready for the next run. The alternative was the throstle, which was a development from the first successful

A nineteenth century engraving of mule spinning; a notable feature is the small boy crawling among the moving machinery.

cotton spinning machine, invented by Richard Arkwright, known as the water frame, because it was powered by a water wheel. In this machine, the threads were stretched by being passed through rollers, moving at different speeds. They then passed down to a rotating flyer to provide the twist. The throstle used the same basic idea but was designed for use with steam power. Because the machines were intended for use with the short staple cotton, it seemed sensible to reduce the silk waste fibres to a similar length for spinning by mule or throstle, but two Glaswegians, John Gibson and John Gordon Campbell, thought otherwise. In 1836, they applied for a patent for what was described as a new or improved process for manufacturing silk.

The patent of 1836 contained descriptions of eight different processes, of which the most important were the descriptions of spinning the long, uncut fibres on an improved throstle, together with spinning in combination with wool or flax. In a further elaboration, the patent described the process as 'the same as that used by flax spinners'. The patent was granted and the yarn became known as 'Patent Long Spin'. As soon as the patent was approved, complaints started to appear, challenging it on the grounds that spinning long waste was not new, but had been carried out for some time. A court case was brought, Gibson v Brand, in which Brand claimed that he had purchased waste silk and sent it away to be spun uncut on a flax spinning machine long before 1836. Eventually, it was agreed by the Court of Common Plea that although it was said that the earlier processes had been carried out in secret, which would not have invalidated the patent, there was sufficient evidence that spinning uncut fibres was a common practice, 'although it had not been carried to such a state of perfection as under the present patent.' As a result, some parts of the patent remained unchanged, and instead of being officially described in the wording as a 'new or improved process' it was now simply 'improved'.

Silk spinners seem to have been a contentious lot. Towards the end of the century, Samuel Cunliffe Lister began manufacturing waste silk imported from India. He was awarded the Albert medal by the Royal Society of Arts for his role in importing waste silk from India and establishing long spinning. This led to his being challenged in a letter in the local paper, signed by 'The Silk Club', which pointed out that others had imported Indian silk and used it before Lister. Lister's reply in March 1887 contains a great deal of fascinating information. He began by agreeing that waste silk had been spun long before he started in business, and that he had not made the claims himself and that the assertions were made by the RSA while he was ill in bed. But he pointed out that the spinning of Indian waste only became profitable due to improvements in machinery.

> I remember well the first time that I saw anything of the kind was at Messrs. Holdforths' mill at Leeds – I think in 1846. Having at that time gained some notoriety in wool-combing, Mr. Holdforth asked me to come over and see his silk-dressing machine, and to improve it if I could. I thought then, and still think, that it was one of the rudest and crudest of machines, but, as I know to my cost, very hard to beat. I had no idea when examining it carefully for the first time, of the long years of toil and trouble, and the ruinous sums it would cost me before I should be able to master it – and I am not sure that I have succeeded even now, after forty years (that is for all sorts) – but I can, at any rate, say that I have, as far as I know, invented and patented the first self-acting dressing machine, with plenty of room for improvement for those who come after me.

Among the other inventions, mentioned in the letter, was the intersecting gill, invented by his partner Mr. Warburton, a machine with two sets of teeth, one above the other, through which the silk was drawn for dressing. He went on to describe how he came to work with waste silk from India. He was shown a sample by a waste silk merchant called Spensley, who thought it worthless – 'he said, laughing, that he had tried to use it as manure, but it would not rot.' He bought a few bales, but once he had finally succeeded in developing the dressing machine, he was buying thousands of bales. When he began manufacturing, he also acquired a loom for weaving velvet, which is created by weaving two layers of fabric at the same time. His original mill burned down in 1871 and its replacement in the Manningham district of Bradford is a mark of just how successful he had become. It was the biggest silk mill in the country, with a floor area of around 27 acres. It was steam powered and the mill chimney still dominates this whole area, rising to an imposing 249 feet. The 32 boilers that supplied the power consumed 1,000 tons of coal a week. At its peak, it employed over 10,000 operatives, mainly women, and continued in operation right through to the end of the twentieth century. Its velvets were particularly sought after, and the company had some notable clients, including King George V and President George Bush, who ordered curtains for the White House. In the Second World War, the mill was kept busy turning out thousands of yards of parachute silk.

At the end of the letter, he complained about the fall in demand, because of the rise in price of the raw material and foreign competition. One particular problem was high tariffs raised against British silk by the American government to protect their own industry. Shortly after Lister wrote his letter to the Silk

Manningham mill, Bradford, that specialised in waste silk spinning and was the biggest silk mill in the country. It has now been converted into apartments.

Club, on 9 December 1889 he posted a notice cutting the wages of large groups of workers which informed them that they could either accept the cuts or be locked out. The workers appealed to the Weavers Textile Association for help and one of their representatives made their case to Lister's. He pointed out that the company had made profits of £138,000 and that the cut in wages would only bring in a modest £7,000 but the affected workers would see their pay cut by a massive 20 per cent. The company refused to accept the argument, and a bitter strike followed. Some 200 blackleg workers were brought in under police escort to carry out little more than essential maintenance work. Meanwhile, the Poor Law Commissioners decreed that strikers could not receive any benefits. The end was inevitable; poverty forced the workers to submit. The strike may have been over, but the dissatisfaction of the workforce had not gone away, and it was felt that they needed to organise themselves to make their voices heard. Shortly after that, the local workers got together to form the Bradford Labour Union. And it was in Bradford that that organisation formed the basis for a brand new political force in Britain – the Independent Labour Party, forerunner of the modern Labour Party. It is somewhat ironic that the country's first socialist party should have had its roots in the country's most luxurious industry.

Lister was not the only one aiming at improvements in the production and quality of waste silk. Because the threads were generally coarser than those from unbroken filaments, they were 'gassed' to remove any unevenness. The threads were passed through a gas flame, which removed any irregularities, which in theory left the silk more lustrous, but unfortunately was also inclined to leave a film of ash, which had exactly the opposite effect, dulling it again. Machine makers from Rochdale, W.H. Prince and James Tomlinson, patented a device for cleaning the silk after gassing, by running it round a number of caps to remove the ash. They sold the rights to Lister's.

The growth of the waste silk industry was helped by a steady reduction in the government tax on the imported raw material, which in 1819 had been as high as £22 a hundredweight but which had reduced to a shilling a hundredweight just ten years later and then dropped altogether. This was reflected in the figures for imports, which in the three years 1815-17 had been 27,000 tons but had risen for 1839-41 to over a million tons. This gives some idea of the growing importance of the waste industry and does not even take account of the waste silk generated by silk throwing mills in Britain. The spun silk was used in a variety of different ways, often to produce comparatively cheap goods which, in the early years, went into bandanas for export, but it could also be used for more luxurious items. Paisley began to use spun silk for its famous shawls and tablecloths.

A very different type of spun silk began to gain popularity towards the end of the nineteenth century. Tussah silk is the product of the wild silk moth of India. This is a quite different species of the genus *Antheraea* and unlike the cultivated moth of China it is not a fussy eater, munching at a wide variety of plants, with a particular fondness for oak leaves. The filaments of the cocoon are lightly coloured and the oak eating worms produce an attractive honey coloured thread. It was not immediately accepted but, in 1872, Sir Thomas Wardle used Tussah, dyed black, to make a silk 'sealskin', which was exhibited at the Paris Exhibition of 1878. It became a very popular line. The machinery first developed in Britain made it possible, and waste spinning soon spread across the world, not just to Europe but also across the Atlantic. The development of the silk industry in America is the next subject and needs a chapter of its own.

CHAPTER TEN

The Americas

The first comprehensive history of the American industry was produced by L.P. Brockett M.D. in 1876, and he at once showed himself to be a thoroughly patriotic citizen. After discussing the early history of silk in Asia then in Europe, his chapter on the American industry begins, 'Silk culture was attempted in the early infancy of the American Colonies, and it is worthy of notice that the first, as well as several of the subsequent efforts to promote it, grew out of the selfish desire of the English kings to keep the colonies dependent on the mother country, and to make them serve its interests, even at the expense of their own.' James I was the immediate object of his scorn.

Earlier on, we looked at the king's unsuccessful attempts to cultivate silk worms in Britain. Brockett links that attempt to the successful cultivation of tobacco in Virginia. The king famously wrote what the American described as a 'most absurd book' – *The Counterblast against Tobacco* – that we now know to be an all too accurate warning that tobacco could damage health. But in Virginia, tobacco was by then so successful that it was, in effect, a currency. Instead of reckoning value in terms of coin, bargainers would think in terms of pounds of tobacco. Now the king wanted to encourage the colonists to abandon tobacco in favour of raising silk worms, in a climate that might be more conducive to success than cold, damp Britain. A peremptory order was made to stop growing tobacco and start planting mulberry trees. The Americans' objection to the scheme was that they were not going to be allowed to manufacture the silk themselves, which could boost the local economy, but instead must send it all off to Britain for processing. They were being asked to abandon a successful and profitable crop for a dubious return. The criticism seems valid. It was in fact just this sort of attitude that Britain's needs must always come first which would eventually lead to the War of Independence.

Whatever the Virginians' opinions might have been, the scheme worked reasonably well. Mulberry trees and silkworms were sent across from Britain in 1623, and legislation that imposed a fine of ten pounds of tobacco on any planter who failed to plant at least ten mulberry trees for every hundred acres of land, ensured that silk production went ahead as planned. The quantities produced were not very large and premiums were offered to increase production. But then the English Civil War broke out with victory going to the Parliamentary forces. Charles I may have had a delight in silks – he wore a silk vest for his execution – but Cromwell and the Puritans were less enthusiastic. The restoration of the monarchy may have brought back an enthusiasm for finery, but interest in Virginia as a source of supply waned. The cultivation of the mulberry trees and raising of silk worms continued to a limited extent, but now instead of being sent abroad, it was woven on the spot – and the richer planters were able to show off their home-made silk waistcoats and handkerchiefs. But it was a small matter, not comparable to the main income which continued to be from tobacco, and according to Brockett, the standard of silk sported by the wealthy was not exactly first class – 'they were imperfect goods, and would be scouted by our beaux and belles as unworthy.' He suggests that the local people did not really understand the intricacies of silk throwing, dyeing and weaving and as a result the silk was coarse, stiff, lacked lustre and did not hold its colours as well.

An attempt to reintroduce silk to America was made in 1732, this time further south in Georgia. Ground was allotted to settlers by the Governor on the condition that they planted 100 white mulberry trees per acre and cultivated them for a minimum of ten years. Plants and seeds were sent from England, together with silkworm eggs, and this time two experts accompanied them; an Episcopalian clergyman who was an expert to advise on rearing the silkworms and a Piedmontese silk reeler. Within three years, the first shipment of eight pounds of raw silk was sent across from Savannah and woven into cloth in England, which was then presented to Queen Caroline. It was a good start, and in 1749, the British government offered further encouragement by removing the taxes on silk from Georgia and the Carolinas and sent over an Italian, Signor Ortolengi, to instruct the Americans on Italian sericulture.

Ortolengi established works at Savannah for reeling, throwing, cleaning and twisting the silk. The initiative was a great success and in 1759, Georgia sent over 10,000 pounds of silk to Britain, which was of such high quality that it fetched a higher price than silk from any other part of the world. The figures are remarkable as, the previous year, the Savannah warehouse had burned down with a considerable quantity of silk and 8,000 pounds of cocoons. It turned out, however, to be a high point. Exports gradually decreased and enthusiasm for silk production diminished; the American South had discovered an alternative and highly profitable crop. Cotton was to dominate the whole economy for years to come.

South Carolina also began producing silk in small quantities, which was said to be of a very high quality. A wealthy lady living near Charleston, Mrs. Eliza Pinckney, had raised silk on her husband's plantation, then had it spun and woven to produce enough material to make three dresses. The family travelled to London in 1755, taking with them the three lengths of silk; one length was presented to Lord Chesterfield, the second to the Dowager Princess of Wales and the third Eliza kept for herself. The family remained in Britain for five years and if she had hoped to arouse interest in South Carolina silk, it seems to have had little effect. As in Georgia, cotton became the staple of the state – as it was to be for much of the South. It was not only simpler to produce than silk, it was an ideal crop for plantations that relied almost entirely on slave labour.

Silk production also began in what was to become the State of Connecticut in the middle of the eighteenth century. Dr N. Aspinwall began planting mulberry trees on Long Island and by 1762 he was sending plants and silk worm eggs to other parts of the state, notably to New Haven and Mansfield. The other great enthusiast was Ezra Stiles, the President of Yale, who worked at putting the cultivation of the mulberry tree and raising of silkworms onto a sound footing, by careful experiments. President George Washington was impressed by the burgeoning silk industry, describing the lustring as 'very good' and the thread as 'very fine'. Mansfield, the town to which Dr Aspinwall had sent one of his first batches of mulberry trees, became a major centre of sericulture and by the early nineteenth century it was estimated that three out of four households in the town were raising silk worms. By 1840, Connecticut was producing three times as much silk as the whole of the rest of the country.

This is quite surprising as the climate of Connecticut is very different from that of the Southern States – in January, the mean temperature is a chilly -3°C. In an article by Taryn Skinner, published in April 2018, a modern sericulturist, Michael Cook, is quoted on what is needed to keep silk moths alive during cold winters. 'Rise early, feed the worms before work, feed them again at lunch, feed them again in the evening and clean a dozen or so big trays, feed them again before bed. I was feeding a garbage bag full of leaves and small branches daily.' The cocoons were generally kept in insulated attics, the best place as warm air rises.

Silk production is a delicate operation and short cuts are seldom effective. When Ezra Stiles introduced mulberry trees, he brought in the Italian variety of white mulberry. The tree grows slowly and has small leaves. To many, it seemed only sensible to switch to the Chinese black mulberry, *M. Multicaulis* which grew faster, had larger leaves and could be harvested more frequently. Investors saw this as an excellent chance to cut the cost of silk rearing and make large profits. Soon, cuttings from the first crop were being sold at ever-increasing prices. Investors were delighted. One man in particular looked to make a fortune. Samuel Whitmarsh, who owned a cocoonery in Massachusetts, started issuing pamphlets praising the value of the black mulberry and made it seem not so much an ordinary plant but a guaranteed perennial money tree. It became a craze and plants were changing hands at ludicrous prices. One of Whitmarsh's associates told the story of a tree that was bought in Massachusetts for $25 and then sold to a farmer in Connecticut for $50, and when he was offered a staggering $450 for a quarter share, turned the offer down. Like so many get rich quick schemes it all ended in disaster.

There were two problems. The first and most obvious one was that the prices being paid for mulberry trees was never sustainable, and in the early 1840s a number of harsh winters and a blight destroyed many trees. The industry might have recovered, but there was a far more fundamental difficulty; the silk from the new mulberry trees was inferior to that of the earlier Italian varieties. It was lumpy and uneven, and the workmanship of the reelers was often poor. The job of reeling the silk from the cocoons went to the women of the household, a job which they had to fit in between their household chores and looking after children. This followed an old established pattern of women spinning at home, which had worked perfectly well, with materials such as wool or cotton, where the spinning could be stopped at any time and taken up again later. It was not a system suited to silk reeling, where constant attention was essential. Unfortunately, the reeling method generally used at first was quite crude. The cocoons were placed in hot water and stirred with a brush. The silk fibres stuck to the brush and were then wound onto a simple hand reel. The threads were often uneven and gummy, and it was said that the threads intended for sewing silk were of such poor quality that they were only sold by barter – no one was prepared to waste money on them. In order to try and improve the quality, a manual was published in Mansfield in 1792, based on a set of instructions written in Piedmont and translated in Britain in 1774-5. It recommended combing the filaments from four cocoons to create two threads, which are then 'twisted round each other, twenty or twenty-five times, that the four ends of each thread may the better join together, crossing one another that your silk may be plump which would otherwise be flat.' A later manual of 1839 suggested a far simpler system, in which the filaments from several cocoons were simply wound together, and when the cocoons were depleted, the ends were tied and only twisted later. As much as half of the silk from the cocoons was ruined and abandoned as waste. Worst of all, the silk was not of a high enough quality for the new silk mills which had been established in Connecticut, first by the Hanks brothers in 1810 in Mansfield. The result was that the market for home reared silk collapsed, and the mulberry trees which had once been so valuable were now virtually worthless. Many farmers went bankrupt, and others simply tore out their mulberry trees and applied the land to more sustainable crops. The bubble had well and truly burst. Brockett summed up the whole situation, neatly if sarcastically:

> The farmers' wives and daughters, when not engaged in feeding the worms, were to reel the silk, and perhaps to spin and twist it, till silk should become as cheap as cotton, and every matron and maid rejoice in the possession of at least a dozen silk dresses. It does not clearly appear where and on what occasions they were to wear these dresses, while their whole time was to be occupied with the care of the silk worms and cocoons.

The debacle effectively wrote an end to silk rearing in America, but not an end to the industry. The silk mills did not go out of business. The mill set up in Mansfield by Horace and Rodney Hanks was the first water powered silk mill in America. It was a tiny, single storey wooden building, with a central door and a window to each side of it and the spinning machinery was crude; the mill building itself has been preserved and is now part of the Greenfield Village Museum in Dearborn, Michigan. It was a start, but hardly a spectacular one, and nothing much happened for the next few years. Then, at

A silk dress worn by Mary Lincoln, the wife of President Lincoln, on display at the Smithsonian Museum of American History.

the end of the 1820s, a young throwster, Edmund Golding, who had been working at a silk mill in Macclesfield, came to America, looking for work. He must have been quite surprised at finding so very little mechanisation in use. A Mansfield businessman 'Alfred Lilly' persuaded Golding to produce drawings showing the machinery used for silk spinning in England. The drawings were comparatively crude, but clear enough to show the working principles. A partnership was formed, the Mansfield Silk Company in 1829, to set up a mill and build machinery for doubling and twisting on the basis of Golding's drawings. The locally produced silk as mentioned earlier was unsuitable, and Golding prevailed on his fellow partners to import raw silk from Britain. It was to set the pattern for future development. Although the raising of silkworms in New England was more or less finished, the American manufacturing industry would grow and develop in the region.

The reeling system was improved thanks to suggestions made by another visiting Englishman, who had a silk tassel business in Boston. In 1830, a Piedmont Reel was bought from France, but it was to be a local man, Nathan Rixford, who developed it and used the process. He had already set up in business at Mansfield Hollow, manufacturing machinery. He suggested improvements to the reeling machinery, and for the very first time it became possible to use native raw silk, and to use it to make a product comparable to that of European manufacturers. Rixford set up his own mill in 1839.

A number of other small mills were built in Mansfield over the next decades, with varying degrees of success. By the time the E.B. Smith Silk Mill was established in 1848, local labour must have been getting scarce, as they found it necessary to use part of the mill building as a boarding house. The Mansfield Silk Company acquired a second, larger mill in 1827 and where the other mills had all concentrated on making thread, they attempted weaving, without much success. Unfortunately, they also invested heavily in the *M. Multicaulis* boom time and, as a result of these two failed ventures, the company became bankrupt. But the largest and most successful Connecticut mill was not built in Mansfield but in Manchester by the three Cheney brothers, Ward, Frank and Rush, with George Wells in 1833. It was a modest two-storey building, just 32 by 45ft and the machinery was water powered. Like many others, they invested in the mulberry tree craze, but had the foresight to get out before the crash, and began importing raw silk from the Far

East. In 1847, Frank Cheney patented the Rixford Roller, with a friction drive that wound the raw silk into double-twisted thread. It was durable and produced far fewer breakages than with earlier threads. The new product was a great success and marked the start of a period of rapid expansion and innovation for the company.

In 1854, Cheney Brothers opened a second factory in Hartford for the manufacture of silk ribbon and the following year they began spinning waste silk. They claimed to be the first in the world to do so, but as seen in the previous chapter, they were far from alone in claiming that honour, though they were certainly the first in America and did not base their machinery on earlier models. The company grew and prospered and by 1860 had 400 employees. Having started the concern with just $50,000 in capital that had now risen to $551,000, the company's growing reputation for innovation attracted a young machinist who had previously worked for the Colt armament manufacturer. Christopher Spencer had invented a new rapid-fire rifle and persuaded Cheney to expand into the arms business. Spencer took his rifle to Washington where he showed it off to Abraham Lincoln, who was so impressed he at once

Silk doubling machinery at the Cheney Brothers factory at Manchester 'Connecticut' photographed during the First World War.

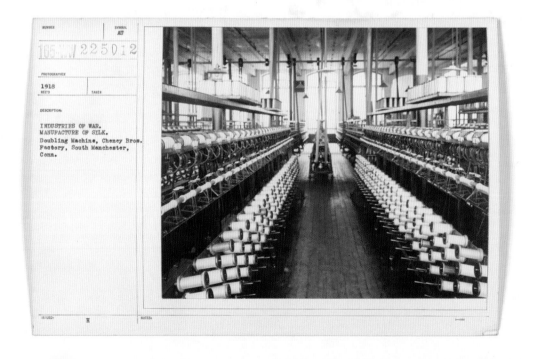

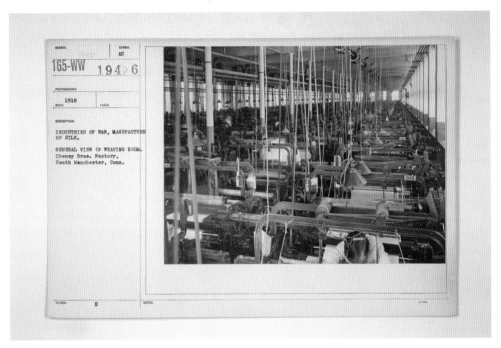

An imposing array of power looms at Cheney Brothers.

Warping a loom at Cheney Brothers.

said that the army could take as many as they could make. Silk, however, remained the core business, and as it expanded so did the company's activities. They built a two mile long railway to link the Manchester and Hartford mills. It also carried passengers. They were very much involved in building the community, supplying houses for the workforce, boasting what at that time was quite a novelty, indoor plumbing. They also built a community centre, churches and schools. They continued innovating with the Grant Reel, which was used for winding the raw silk in a criss-cross pattern that avoided snagging. It was a huge success and was soon in use in factories around the world. In the 1920s, the concern was immense with a work force of 4,700. It seemed a story of continuing success and expansion, and in 1923 recorded a massive profit of $23 million, but like so many other industries it struggled to survive in the great depression following the Wall Street crash of 1929. We shall return to their story again later, but there is one other interesting aspect of the Cheney story that should be mentioned. The Cheney brothers had a reputation for being good employers. Brockett states that the girls who formed the majority of the workforce were treated as equals and there is further evidence of the nature of the Cheney family in the next generation. Charles Cheney was an enthusiastic abolitionist, and his home was one of the stations on the famous Underground Railroad. Runaway slaves were often hidden there – at considerable risk to the family.

The end of silkworm rearing in the north east did not mark the end of the industry as a whole. The sensible decision was made to breed the moths in the warmer climates further south, initially in California and then in Louisiana. There was an incentive not just to produce for American manufacturers, but the possibility of serving a wider market. In an article in *The Scientific American* in July 1869, it was reported that Italy had paid 50 million francs to Japan for cocoons and was offering a premium of 50,000 francs for anyone who could provide quality eggs at a good price. One Louisiana firm at Covington, Louisiana, had been very successful and was producing cocoons at 150 per pound and between March and April had around a million for sale. A sample had been sent to Italy in the hopes of gaining the premium.

The Cheney brothers were by no means the only successful company to set up mills in the northern states. An excellent example which has left us a reminder of its importance in the shape of one of America's most imposing silk mills began with the Belding brothers who were initially simply selling silk thread in a town then known as Broas Rapids, but later named Belding to honour the family which had brought prosperity to the town. The business became so successful that they decided to start manufacturing and established their first mill at Rockville, Connecticut, in 1866. The venture was so successful that they soon added other mills in Massachusetts, California and Montreal. Then, in 1886, the brothers returned to their home town and built a substantial mill. Then, for some reason, they felt that they had perhaps overstretched themselves and sold it to George Richardson, their office manager. Whatever doubts the Beldings may have had, the mill was an immediate success, so the brothers began building again in the town, adding three new mils in the 1890s. Meanwhile, Richardson expanded his mill, which the Belding brothers repurchased in 1910. It continued in business until 1932. Today, the imposing building has been converted into apartments. It is not the only reminder of the importance of the Belding family. They built dormitories for the unmarried women who worked in the mill, and one of these, the Belrackton Dormitory, still survives. A neo-classical building, it is now home to the Belding Museum.

The mills of the northern states continued to prosper, mainly water powered. William Skinner opened his Unquomonk Silk Mill in Haydenville, Mass. Like other mills in the area, it relied for its water supply on the reserves held in the Williamsburg reservoir on the Mill River. On 16 May 1874, the reservoir burst its banks and an

The imposing Richardson silk mill at Belding, Michigan.

Winding silk from skeins onto bobbins at Sir William Skinner & Sons, Holyoke, Massachusetts.

estimated 6 million tons of water flowed out. The Skinner mill was only one of the mills in the area that were completely destroyed, and 148 people lost their lives. The mill was one of the largest in the country, so that its total destruction gives an idea of the sheer force of the deluge. Many of the mill workers who survived found their homes and possessions had also been swept away. A relief fund was set up to help the operatives. Girls received $100 dollars each and a trunk of clothing. Single men got $50 each and clothing; tenants $300 and householders an additional $500. Skinner at once set about rebuilding the mill in an elaborate Italianate style, and it was back in business in 1875.

In spite of the successes in raising silkworms in California and Louisiana, most American manufacturers preferred to import the raw silk from either China or Italy. Although the Italian imports towards the end of the nineteenth century were generally two dollars a pound dearer than the Chinese, the Chinese had far more imperfections and waste, so that in the long run the Italian was actually better value. The method of treatment varied between Chinese and Italian batches. The process began the same for both types, which was sorting by degree of fineness. A parcel of sorted skeins is then placed in cotton bags and soaked in water at about 110°F (42°C) for a few hours, then placed in a perforated cylinder, which is rapidly turned by steam, acting as a centrifuge to force out the water. The Italian is now ready for use, but the Chinese would normally need an extra process of being passed through a cleaning machine, where sharp blades remove imperfections. After that, this silk too is ready for throwing.

In the early years, American manufacturing processes were less sophisticated than those of Europe, and in many accounts there are stories of workmen who arrived from Europe to help set up mills and advise on machinery. It was inevitable, however, that as the industry grew, the Americans would begin making improvements of their own. The industry had received something of a boost in the 1860s. The Civil War may have cost countless lives and caused swathes of devastation, but it helped the local silk industry. With so much money being poured into the war, there was little available for exotic imports. Currency was scarce. So high tariffs were set for imported silk cloth. The demand was still there, and the home industry expanded to meet it. Among the earliest successes was the throwing machine built by the Danforth Locomotive & Machine Co. This was an immense machine; the first they built was 32ft long and had 684 spindles. It turned at speeds up to 8,000 revolutions a minute, and ran so smoothly that it only required two operatives. They also built a ribbon loom that could weave 28 ribbons per loom.

By the end of the nineteenth century, silk had become an important industry in the northern states and mill towns grew up much as they had in Britain, dominated by large mills and housing

Company housing for silk workers in Lancaster, Pennsylvania; the houses were all let at moderate rents.

that often clustered round the industrial buildings. Accommodation varied between the boarding houses for the many single girls and young women who made up much of the workforce, such as the dormitory buildings of Belding. Other mill companies built houses that could be rented by workers' families at comparatively modest cost and often built to a high standard, such as those in Lancaster, Pennsylvania.

Power looms had long since replaced the old hand looms, but as in other parts of the world, inventors were looking for a more efficient way of passing the weft thread across the warp than by shuttle. One of the successful versions was the Earnshaw needle loom as improved by J.H. Greenleaf and manufactured at the famous Colt factory. It was based to some extent on the sewing machine, in that the weft was carried by eye-pointed needle at the end of an iron rod. Instead of throwing the shuttle, the rod was driven through the shed by a crank and, at the far side the thread is disconnected and the rod returns. It was not unlike the rapier loom, the first version of which was developed in Britain by John Smith of Salford in 1844.

Transferring the warp from a large reel to the beam at the back of the loom at a mill in South Manchester, Connecticut, c. 1914.

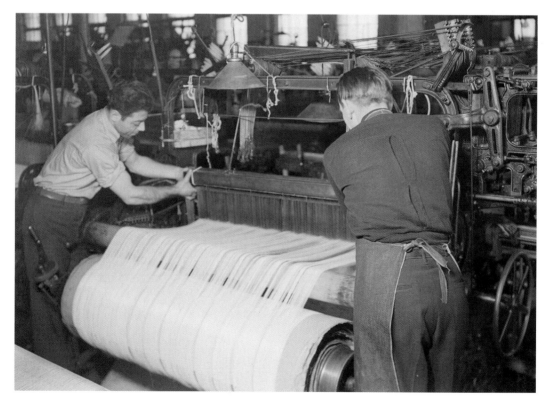

It took some time for the American silk industry to establish itself, and in some areas it had to rely entirely on imported machinery. One of these areas was the manufacture of lace. The lace-making machinery was brought over from Nottingham, the main centre for lace making in Britain, where machinery had been developed from the earlier stocking frame – which was just as its name suggests. The earliest machines invented by John Heathcoat were operated by handles and foot pedals, but later versions worked by power were introduced into Heathcoat's factory in 1818. The machinery was expensive and, for complex patterns, a Jacquard attachment also had to be imported. The local industry was so new that when bobbins broke, they had to be sent back to England for repair. As with other branches of the silk industry, the lace makers soon learned to stand on their own two feet. But the industry was never as important as other textile industries, mostly manufacturing silk cloth and velvet. Silk might be called the queen of fabrics, but in America, Cotton was King.

CHAPTER ELEVEN

Science and Silk

The study of chemistry, as opposed to alchemy, goes back to the eighteenth century and was often the work of amateurs. Joseph Priestley 'who first isolated oxygen' was a non-conformist minister, while Antoine Lavoisier, who also worked with oxygen and showed that water was made up of hydrogen and oxygen, was a French aristocrat. Great advances were made well into the early part of the nineteenth century in the understanding of chemical composition and in that time an important split was made in the subject. It was discovered that there was a vast range of substances based on carbon, many of which were found in naturally growing substances. This branch of chemistry became known as 'organic' for that reason, and everything else was 'inorganic'. The current use of the word 'organic' in describing, for example, food, is somewhat misleading, since to a chemist virtually all food is organic. There was not necessarily anything obvious in the physical appearance of organic compounds to distinguish them from inorganic substances. How many of us has at some time or other mistakenly put salt in a cup of tea instead of sugar? Yet common salt, sodium chloride, is inorganic, each molecule made up of a single atom of sodium joined to one of chlorine, while a molecule of the usual table sugar is made up of 12 carbon atoms, 22 hydrogen atoms and 11 oxygen atoms. There is a clue here as to why organic substances were the ones scientists began to make use of for developing all kinds of new compounds – they are generally far more complex than their inorganic relations, and can be arranged in an almost infinite series of combinations with just a few basic elements. What has all this to do with silk? Well the dyes used up to now in the industry were all made from natural products, such as saffron for yellow and indigo for blue, and were therefore organic. They were, however, very complex – far too complex for anyone initially to even contemplate trying to reproduce these dyes artificially, though there was an obvious case for doing so. Some of the natural dyes, notably the yellows, were difficult to produce consistently. Manufacturers would have loved to have had better dyes, but no one, it seemed, knew how to produce them. But an artificial dye was eventually produced, and the story of how it happened is an intriguing one.

August Wilhelm von Hofmann was born at Giessen in Germany in 1818 and initially studied law and philosophy but soon became fascinated by chemistry. In 1845, he was appointed superintendent of the newly formed Royal College of Chemistry in London. He realised that coal tar was a very useful and widely available source for a variety of organic compounds. Some of them at least could be separated out by partial distillation. Basically, different constituents have different boiling points so that by careful work, the compound with the lowest boiling point could be removed first, then the next and so on. It opened up all kinds of possibilities, which made it a very appealing area of study for eager young scientists who signed up as Hofmann's assistants – too enthusiastic in one case. Charles Mansfield was so keen to continue experimenting that he set up his own lab in his lodgings and, while he was distilling, the apparatus he was using caught fire; the unfortunate young chemist died in the blaze.

One of the substances that Hofmann isolated from coal tar was benzene which had been mixed with nitric acid to produce a yellowish oil, which could then be further reduced to form a substance called aniline; the name comes from the Portuguese word 'anil' or indigo. Indigo is, of course, one of the many dyes that manufacturers hoped to replace, but that was not what interested the scientists. They developed a new compound which they called allyl-toluidine that had a structure remarkably like quinine. This was definitely of interest as quinine was an important medicine – it was essential in the treatment of malaria, a disease all too common in various parts of what was then the widespread British Empire. Another of Hoffman's bright young men, William Perkin, began experimenting with ways of producing artificial quinine. The allyl-toluidine was composed of atoms of carbon, hydrogen and nitrogen, but quinine also had an oxygen atom attached, and to make a molecule identical to the original he had to make other adjustments.

Perkin treated his allyl-toluidine with potassium dichromate, which he hoped would add the extra oxygen, and sulphuric acid. All he got was a muddy reddish-brown substance that was definitely not quinine. It was a setback, but he persevered, and this time started with aniline. It looked just as unpromising – a black sludge. He tried boiling it with water and found that some of it dissolved, producing a purplish liquid that could be crystallised as it cooled. It still wasn't quinine, but the colour was attractive and then he took an imaginative step. He decided to see if he could use it to dye silk. The result was satisfactory; the cloth turned an attractive light, purplish colour, which didn't disappear when the cloth was washed and showed no sign of fading. He sent a sample to a leading firm of dyers, Pullars of Perth, and received this encouraging reply, quoted in the Oxford University Press *History of Technology* Vol. V. 1958:

> If your discovery does not make the goods too expensive, it is decidedly one of the most valuable that has come out for a very long time. This colour is one which has been very much wanted in all classes of goods, and could not be obtained fast on silks, and only at great expense on cotton yarns. I enclose for you a pattern of the *best* lilac we have on cotton – it is dyed by only one house in the United Kingdom, but even then it is not quite fast, and does not stand the tests that yours does, and fades by exposure to air. On silk the colour has always been fugitive.

It was the first aniline dye. Not surprisingly, Perkin was keen to cash in on his discovery and with the help of his father, who put up the finance, and his brother, who was a builder, they opened a factory near Harrow in 1857. At this time, the dye was known rather unromantically as 'aniline purple', and proved very successful for dyeing silk, but less so, initially, for use with cotton. It became very popular in France, where it was renamed 'mauve', a name that stuck. Although the attempt to gain a French patent failed, its popularity in that country had its effect in Britain – as fashions from France have done for many years. The greatest publicity the new colour got came when Queen Victoria turned up at the Great Exhibition in the Crystal Palace in a mauve silk dress. The craze for the new colour grew so rapidly, that it even made it into a *Punch* cartoon, with a policeman ordering spectators to 'get a mauve on'. The dye was such a financial success that Perkin was able to retire and devote himself to chemistry research, and eventually to be knighted as Sir William Perkin. He continued to work with dyes and other researchers were soon producing a wide range of synthetic dyes.

If an alternative to naturally occurring plant dyes could be manufactured, many researchers began to wonder whether it might also be possible to manufacture an artificial cloth, and

An early twentieth century English mauve silk dress worn by the donor's aunt Phyllis Whitworth and now in the Auckland Museum.

the obvious candidate was the luxury, expensive material, silk. A logical place to start seemed to be the mulberry tree. Surely if a simple creature like the silkworm could make the filaments by chewing mulberry leaves, an intelligent scientist should be able to find a way of transforming the same plant into a silky fabric. It was a swiss chemist, George Audamans, who tried first. He took the inner bark of the mulberry tree, mixed it with a solvent, and then used a needle to draw out the gummy mixture into threads, which he described as 'artificial silk'. It was a slow, clumsy process and in this little contest between clever scientist and not very bright silkworm, the silkworm emerged a clear winner. However, the process was patented, even though it was never taken up commercially. Sir Joseph Swan also tried using bark to create artificial silk, but he used a very different method of production, creating threads by forcing the material through small holes, a technique that was to be further developed and used in later experiments. The Swan method, however, was no more commercially successful than Audamans'.

Others took a different line, deciding that it was unlikely that the mulberry tree had any specific property, but there might be a fundamental element present in all green plants that might be the basis for experiments. There was, indeed, just such a material: cellulose. This consists of long chains of glucose units, which form the main constituent of plant cells, giving plants the strength to stand upright. It proved a promising starting point for producing new substances. The first important step was taken by a professor at Basle University, Christopher Frederick Schönhein, who treated paper with nitric and sulphuric acids to create cellulose nitrate, the starting point for the production of several new materials, the first plastics.

Alexander Parkes was born in Birmingham in 1813 and was apprenticed to a brass founder before getting a job with the Elkington company, who had patented electroplating. He was clearly both ambitious and talented, for, by 1841, he had taken out the first of several patents, this one for electroplating delicate objects. The technique was used at Elkington's and when Prince Albert visited in 1844, he was presented with a silver-plated spider's web. He was to go on to produce a number of inventions, but it was not until the mid-1850s that he turned his attention to what might be done with cellulose nitrate. He was very aware of the need for a new form of electrical insulation to replace the natural materials then in use, such as gutta percha. He tried a variety of different solvents with the cellulose nitrate, until he finally produced a material that he felt was ideal for the job, and he also discovered that it had another use as a waterproofing material. He named it 'parkesine' and exhibited it at the Crystal Palace Exhibition of 1862. By 1866, he had set up a factory at Hackney Wick, but the material was not a success; it proved to be brittle and expensive and the company was wound up. But what he had produced was the first usable plastic and others were soon finding other applications.

Daniel Spill had originally trained as a doctor but joined his brother George in a company producing waterproof sheeting by spreading rubber over cloth. He became interested in parkesine and was appointed manager of the Hackney works. When that venture ended, he continued experimenting with cellulose nitrate, to produce new plastics that he called 'ivonide' and 'xylonite'. This was to be the centre of protracted arguments over patents, as a very similar product was being developed at the same time in America by John Wesley Hyatt.

The next development was all down to a sporting problem in America; a shortage of ivory for billiard balls. One of the leading manufacturers offered an award of $10,000 for anyone who could come up with a good quality artificial ivory. As mentioned above, Spill had obviously been on the right track with his ivonide, but it was John Wesley Hyatt who, acting quite independently, set to work to win the prize. He treated cellulose nitrate with a variety of different compounds before eventually finding the ideal combination – camphor in ethanol. His brother came up with a name based on the original natural foundation of the plastic – he called it celluloid. It had a wide range of uses, one of the most popular of which was for making cuffs for clerks. It would protect their shirts from ink smears, and the celluloid could simply be wiped clean. We have finally arrived back at a material with a connection with the garment industry, though not exactly hitting the high fashion mark – elegant ladies did not get ink stains on their clothes. Hyatt and Spill were to contest their respective patents over the years, the courts first favouring Spill and then Hyatt. But what was clear was that polymers really could be manufactured to serve many different purposes. A series of events that had begun with an attempt to make artificial silk had ended with a revolution in the manufacture of other materials, and set in motion the age of plastics; an age which had once seemed a boon, but has become an international menace. What had not yet appeared was a satisfactory way to produce any thread resembling silk.

The shortage of ivory encouraged the development of the first plastics. Now, in the 1870s, there was a threat to silk production in France because of an epidemic that was destroying the silkworms. This was to lead to the first successful attempt to make artificial silk. One of the leading scientists of the day, Louis Pasteur, was one of many trying to tackle the problem. Working with him was a young aristocratic engineer, Louis-Marie Hilaire Bernigaut de Grange, Comte de Chardonnet. Pasteur managed to identify that the problem came from a parasite that infected the mulberry leaves and the worms that fed on them. He recommended destroying the existing stock and starting again with unaffected plants and worms. This solved the problem and Pasteur moved on to other great works. Chardonnet, however, had become fascinated with the silkworms and began experimenting, though with little initial success. Then he had an accident in the lab.

Nitro cellulose had proved a versatile material, and one form was used to create gun cotton. In 1846, Louis Menard dissolved gun cotton in a mixture of ether and alcohol. When the solution evaporated, he was left with a transparent, colourless liquid that dried to form a thin, colourless film, which was called collodion. This was used to coat and protect photographic plates. One day, when Chardonnet was working in the dark room, he accidentally knocked over a bottle of liquid collodion. He took a cloth to clean it up, and as he wiped the material, it began to form long filaments. He at once saw their similarity to silk threads and began a new series of experiments with nitro cellulose, the basic material of collodion. He did as earlier researchers had done, and used cellulose from mulberry leaves as a starting point. He produced a glutinous solution that he squeezed through a plate with small perforations to produce a thread that could be spun and woven. It was a process that took a long time to develop, but in 1889 he was able to exhibit a new material – 'Chardonnet silk' – at the Paris Exhibition. It was lustrous and attractive and the public were enthusiastic. Soon finance was available and the new material went into production in 1891. It was eventually given a new name and someone suggested that as it shimmered with rays of light it might be called 'Rayon'. It was a success, but in its earliest form was highly inflammable. The factory workers had their own name for the material, a rather black joke; they called it 'mother-in-law silk' – the ideal gift for an unloved, interfering lady who, with luck, might go up in flames. Later, production methods were improved and the material made safe.

In 1894, British chemist Charles Frederick Cross, with his associates Edward John Bevan and Clayton Beadle, produced a new type of artificial silk, which they named 'viscose', because it came from a viscous solution. In this process, the cellulose, now mostly obtained from wood pulp, was treated with carbon disulphide and hydrogen peroxide. This would later become known as viscose rayon and was first commercially produced in Britain by Courtaulds in 1905.

The process that was eventually developed there started at the pulp mill, where spruce logs were stripped of their bark, broken into small pieces and boiled with sodium bisulphite. It was then washed, shredded and compressed into sheets of wood pulp. These were then sent to the manufacturer, where they were weighed and soaked in caustic soda. After steeping for a carefully measured length of time, the sheets were squeezed to remove the caustic soda, and then kneaded into cellulose crumbs, which was then churned

Artificial silks for weaving manufactured in Britain.

An English rayon dress from c.1940 in the Auckland Museum.

with sodium disulphide to form cellulose xanthate or viscose. After this had been allowed to age, it was forced under pressure into a spinning machine, which had many small holes in a spinarette. The viscose emerged from the holes into an aqueous solution, where it appeared as a continuous filament, and was then wound onto a wheel, turning at a steady speed. It was then passed to a second wheel, running faster than the first to draw out the filament. The idea of using rollers at different speeds takes us right back to the eighteenth century, when Richard Arkwright used the same idea to stretch cotton in his pioneering water frame for spinning. The filament was now fed into a rotating box, which provides twist and the centrifugal force drives the twisted threads to the outside of the box. Once the twisted thread had been dried with hot air, it was ready for use.

The fibre had one great advantage over the Chardonnay rayon – it was not flammable, which was obviously good news for mothers-in-law. Courtaulds would later open a plant in America. Rayon fibres are still produced in vast quantities, and the latest figures show an annual production of 5.8 million tons, two thirds of which is made in China. Artificial silk has come a long way, but it has never had the allure and magic of the natural fibre. But at its best, it made a material that had at least the appearance of silk available to many who could never have afforded the real thing.

CHAPTER TWELVE

Silk in the Modern World

When we last looked at the industry in America, it was still dominated by the Cheney Brothers mills, the company was thriving – and it continued to grow and prosper. A whole new set of mill buildings was constructed between 1872 and 1917. By 1920, they were employing nearly 5,000 workers, a quarter of the population of Manchester, Connecticut. They dominated the town, supplying electricity and gas, building the local fire station and schools and were notably good employers, providing pensions and medical care. Other companies were doing equally well. This did not, however, mean that the mill workers were doing equally well. Between 1909 and 1919, there were a number of strikes in silk mills, of which the most famous took place at Paterson, New Jersey. They were encouraged by the success of a strike in Lawrence, Massachusetts, that had resulted in workers receiving a rise in wages. The Paterson workers had a long list of grievances: wages had been declining, working days were long and conditions poor. The mills were looking to improve productivity by modernisation and wanted to introduce a new system for weavers, where one operative could look after as many as four looms. The movement was led at first by the militant ribbon weavers who looked for help from the Socialist organisation, Industrial Workers of the World (IWW). When the demands of the workers were ignored, the strike began on 25 February.

From the start, it was clear that this was a strike about politics as much as industrial relations, at least as far as the authorities were concerned. On the first day, one of the IWW leaders, Elizabeth Gurley Flynn, gave a speech urging the workforce to unite, ignoring all differences of race and national origins. She was promptly arrested. Within a short time, all the IWW representatives who came to Paterson were also arrested. But it made no difference to the strike. The local workers had their own organisation, and the full force of the law was brought to bear; before it was over, almost 2,000 workers had been arrested. There was to be a final defiant gesture, when the workers organised and performed in a great

Part of the immense Barnett silk mill at Paterson, New Jersey, photographed in 1937. The industrial buildings tower over the workers' houses.

pageant, but ultimately, they were simply unable to survive with no wages coming in. The strike ended on 28 July. In one sense, it was a battle that could never have been won as long as the strikers were opposing the introduction of the new regime for the looms. It was inevitable that Paterson would have to do as other mills were already doing or lose out to the competition. But the other demands for good working conditions, an 8-hour day and reasonable pay were all too justified but were never met. The defeat of the Paterson strike also saw a decline in the membership of the IWW, though it still exists. But in America the emphasis shifted to less militant labour unions.

The years of widespread strikes in the silk industry ended and the early 1920s were an especially good time thanks to a change in fashions. Hem lines were on the rise and ladies did not want to be seen with bare legs, and quite the most prestigious covering was the silk stocking. The one big difference between this period in the early days of the industry was that the manufacturers in America no longer looked to other Americans to provide the raw material, but turned back to the Far East, and in particular to Japan.

It is not certain when silk was first produced in Japan, but it seems to have arrived via Korea in the fourth century. Printed silk has survived from the eighth century palace at Nara, once the capital of Japan. Soon, it became common practice for Japanese women to rear silkworms in the attics of their houses. The importance of sericulture was emphasised by a custom, still preserved, that each spring the Empress of Japan feeds the silkworms in the palace gardens. In time, the Japanese perfected sericulture to the point where the quality of the silk they produced was the finest in the world, surpassing China, where it had all begun. The secret lay in the care and attention to detail.

Japanese workers at the Corticelli Co in America, removing newly hatched silkworms from the egg paper and feeding them.

In modern Japanese sericulture, the silkworms are raised in trays, in rooms kept at a steady temperature of 24 to 27°C, in a room where the lights are permanently kept on but never shine directly on the caterpillars. Cleanliness is vital and the women of Hangzhou who raise silkworms are forbidden to smoke, wear make up and, rather oddly, eat garlic. According to the web site factsanddetails.com the Japanese follow the rules laid down in China centuries ago.

FEEDING THE YOUNG SILKWORMS AND REMOVING FROM THE EGG PAPERS THE TINY CORTICELLI SILKWORMS JUST HATCHED.

First of all, the bark of a dog, even a foul smell can upset freshly hatched worms. Second, larvae should rest on dry mattresses, and they must sleep, eat and work in harmony. Third, a worm out of sync with the rhythm and transformation of the majority is buried or fed to fish to avoid any variation in the silk. Fourth, drowsy newly hatched worms are tickled with a chicken feather to prod development. And finally, the attendant, called silkworm mother, should have no bad smells, should wear clean, simple clothes so as not to stir the air and should not eat chicory or even touch it.

The production of these pampered little beasts was almost all carried out in people's homes, and in the main silk production district of Gumma, there was in its peak period 25,000 of such homes. One of the main customers for Japanese silk was France in the nineteenth century, and it was from Japan that fresh silk worms were supplied after Pasteur had identified the parasite that had affected local stocks. In the 1920s, the American silk stocking manufacturers relied almost entirely on Japanese silk.

In the latter part of the nineteenth century, the Meiji dynasty was restored in Japan, and it was decided that it was time for the country

A Japanese silk merchant displaying his wares to potential customers in 1893.

to try to catch up with the West by a process of industrialisation. Silk was already a major export, but was still based on domestic production, which made it difficult to keep to standards. The government decided that the answer would be the construction of a modern mill complex. The man in charge of the project was Shibusawa Eiichi from the Ministry of Finance, a bureaucrat but one who came from a family who were engaged in sericulture, so understood the problems. With no local experience of modern silk technology, a technical expert was needed, and the job of technical overseer went to Paul Brunat, a Frenchman involved in the silk trade in Yokohama. Working alongside him was Odaka Junchu, who was later to become manager of the mill. The site chosen was Tomioka, where there was an existing domestic silk industry and local coal mines for fuel. The actual construction was entrusted to another Frenchman, Edmond Auguste Bastien. Its appearance, not surprisingly, owed very little to Japanese traditional styles or construction methods. Bastien used timber framing with brick infill and glazed windows. Locals had to be taught how to produce the bricks in the first place, but it marked the beginning of brick manufacture on a large scale in the country. An indication of the degree of the change from Eastern to Western building ideas can be gauged from the fact that the windows had to be brought over from France, machinery was imported from Lyon, and experts came over from France to help set up the machinery and train operatives. They had their own special dormitory block in the complex.

Work began in March 1871 and when the mill opened in July 1872, it was an imposing array, with two big cocoon warehouses and the actual silk reeling mill contained 300 French machines of the latest design. Everything was in place but there was no work force. The idea had been to employ mainly women, but at first none came forward. There was no experience of factory work, and the insular Japanese were more than a little wary of the foreigners who had come to the site with Brunat. The French, not surprisingly, were often to be seen enjoying glasses of red wine with their meals and rumours spread that the foreign devils drank human blood. However, when Odaka Junchu's daughter volunteered to work in the new factory, other women were persuaded that there was no real problem after all, and recruitment began in earnest. It was not only ordinary workers who were required, but also women who could be trained in the new technology and then go out to teach others. Teaching was an acceptable occupation, and young women

The Empress of Japan visiting the newly opened Tomioka silk mill.

from high ranking, including Samurai, families came to the mill. The locals called them 'silk princesses'.

The women who came to the mill lived in dormitories in groups of twenty, each group with its own supervisor. They worked six days a week, with long hours, but had Sundays off – though they were expected to use the day to do their laundry. Discipline was strict. It was rare for the women to be allowed out of the compound and during the working day, talking was strictly forbidden. When they first arrived, the women worked in the cocoon room, which was steamy and unpleasantly smelly. They were then moved into the factory for reeling, which was something they all looked forward to. When they were moved depended on the overseer. One worker, Yokota Ei, wrote a diary of her time at the mill, and she

Inside a Japanese silk factory c. 1910, one of a series of tinted plates showing different aspects of Japanese life. The women are drawing the silk filaments from the cocoons.

recalled her dismay when all the girls from her region were left in the cocoon room, while a group from another district who arrived later was moved on. It was the district from which the overseer himself had originated. The women protested and were moved on – the supervisor blaming the 'mistake' on the foreigners. As they learned the business, the women were eventually graded as first, second, third class or unclassified workers. The higher grades got better pay, ranging from 18 yen a month for first class to 6 yen for unclassified. Not surprisingly, Yokota Ei wrote that when she was classified as first class, 'I was seized with such joy that the tears poured down'. On the whole, working conditions were tough, but the women were well treated, receiving a regular clothing allowance for summer and winter clothes, good food and medical care – with the prospects of a good career ahead of them. Many went back to their hometowns, where new mills were being built, and began the training processes there.

Once it had achieved its prime function of training staff who could help spread the new technology, the government sold the mill to the Misui family in 1893. After that, it passed to the Hara Company, which in turn was incorporated into the Katakura Silk Spinning Co., the biggest manufacturer of raw silk in the country. It finally closed in 1987 and was donated to the city in 2014 to be preserved and has now been recognised as a UNESCO World Heritage site.

Another important development in Japan was the work of Chogoro Takayaha, born in 1830. As a young man he became interested in sericulture and developed the Seion-Iku system, which relied on good ventilation and temperature control for the cocoons, together with cold storage for the eggs. He founded the Takayaha-Sha school of sericulture, which promulgated his ideas and became a major teaching institute not just for Japanese students but for many who came from abroad. It has now joined the silk mill as a World Heritage Site.

Apart from a vital export market, there was an equally important demand for silk for the upper classes. The traditional dress, the kimono, is ideally suited for extravagant decoration. The emperor and the court had initially relied heavily on imported silk, but that was no longer necessary. Although the garment has a long history, the name 'kimono' is comparatively modern, and though it seems exotic to the West, it simply means 'thing to be worn', simply because it was worn by both men and women, unlined in summer, lined in winter. One reason why it lends itself so well to decoration is that it is made from a single roll of cloth and held together by a sash or 'obi'. Unlike western fashions, the actual shape scarcely changed through the ages – everything was in the design. The higher the social class, the more elaborate the decoration, whether embroidered or printed. The kimono carried elaborate messages, with motifs having symbolic significance – the crane for example signified longevity. There were also social messages. A woman might wear a kimono with references to literature, which told the world she was a lady with leisure for reading. In the 1930s, nationalistic Japan began producing extraordinary kimonos for young boys covered with militaristic motifs, from battleships to fighter planes. The finest kimonos, however, are true works of art.

The important export industry of raw silk to America began to suffer in the 1920s. The Japanese manufacturers responded initially by cutting wages to the point where they were half those earned by silk manufacturers in France and Italy. But the biggest blow came with the introduction of a new material developed in America.

Rayon had been introduced to the world as 'artificial silk', but the truth was that it was at best a poor relation. Several companies set to work to try and produce a better version. One of these was the grand E.L. du Pont de Nemours who in 1920 bought a 60 per cent share in a French rayon company for $4 million. The company name was changed to the more manageable, plain du Pont. They spent a great deal of money in research to improve the quality of rayon, in particular trying to make it softer – in one year alone the research budget was a massive million dollars. The initial results were not very reassuring. In 1926, the head of the Du Pont chemical division, Charles Stine, sent out a memo suggesting that the whole approach was wrong. They were trying to improve an existing material, when what they should be doing was finding a new, better one. And the way to do that was to open a laboratory devoted to 'pure' scientific research. The idea was approved, and Stine was authorised to hire twenty-five top chemists for a new facility with a budget of $25,000 a month, roughly $365,000 at today's prices.

There was some reluctance among top chemists, understandably suspicious that a very commercial company would not, in practice, tie their research to practical and profitable results. However, a young organic chemist, William H. Carothers, joined the company from Harvard University. He set about a programme of fundamental

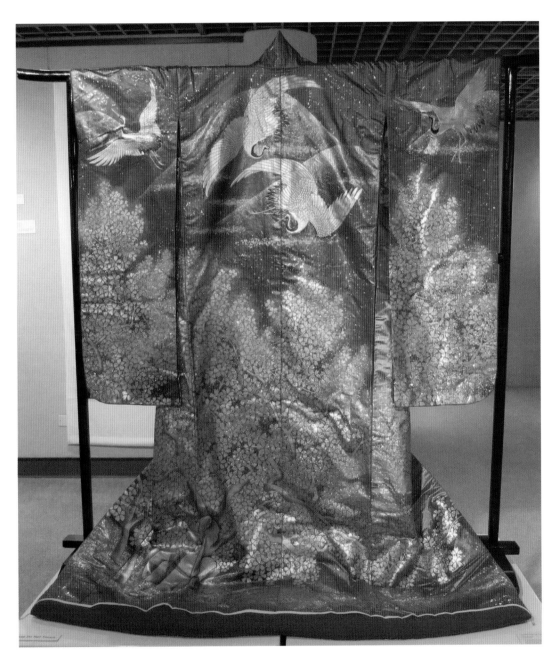

research into the nature of polymers. One current theory suggested they were colloids – very small particles distributed evenly through another medium. An alternative version proposed that they were composed of very long molecules, consisting of a chain of atoms. The latter was the view held by Carothers and he set out to prove

An elaborate Japanese silk kimono with a 'tree of life' motif.

it. He took a series of short organic molecules and began adding them together. In 1930, one of Carothers' associates produced a long polymer by combining an alcohol with an acid – the first polyester. What at once attracted attention was the fact that the brittle fragments formed when the mixture cooled could be extended to four times their original length and became much more elastic. They had no immediate commercial value, as these polymers had a very low melting point – which, apart from being dangerous meant they were impossible to iron without disintegrating. But it showed that this was a fruitful area to investigate.

Four years of research produced nothing viable; new materials either had a low melting point, were soluble in water or both. Carothers was persuaded to take up the challenge, and this time instead of working with polyesters, he changed to working with polyamides. These are also long chain polymers, but they contain the amide group, consisting of one atom of nitrogen and two of hydrogen, derived from ammonia. In May 1934, a member of the team, Donald Coffman, produced a fibre with all the advantages of the polyesters but none of the problems. It was not quite the ideal product yet but by 1938, the new material was ready to go into manufacture. Du Pont decided to concentrate on limiting this material to a single use – making ladies' stockings. This was a huge market, and America was already paying over $70 million a year for Japanese silk to meet the demand. The cheap end of the market was met by the less satisfactory rayon. All that was needed now was a catchy name. The first suggestion was 'Nuron', which was no run spelled backwards, which was obviously a good selling point, but there were copyright problems. The next suggestion was 'Nilon', but as there was ambiguity as to how the I would be pronounced – as in 'mind' or in 'kiss', the I was changed to a y. The new material became Nylon.

Nylon was a huge success, but production at first was limited. It was officially launched in October 1938, and the first 4,000 pairs of stockings were snapped up. It took time to go into full production and when the stockings eventually became widely available at a bargain price of $1.15 a pair, stores had sold out by noon on the first day. In 1940, Du Pont sold $9 million worth of nylon yarn and that shot up to $25 million the following year. This was excellent news for Du Pont, but disaster for the Japanese silk manufacturers. A rumour spread in Japan that it was all an American plot to attack their industrial growth, and the name was really an acronym; Now you laugh on Nippon.

De verkoop van
Nylon KOUSEN
Vindt plaats op 9 *Aug: as*

*Deze kousen worden
alleen aan* DAMES
verkocht.

*De toewijzing
zal bij* LOTING
geschieden

When war broke out between America and Japan, nylon was to find other uses – notably in making parachute silk and flak jackets. Stockings were scarce, particularly in Britain, where young women were often reduced to drawing the iconic and flattering dark seam up the backs of their legs, A visiting GI soon found that a pair of nylons was a far more welcome calling card than a bunch of roses. When the war ended, Du Pont went into full production to provide yarn for stockings, and when they came on the market there were 'nylon riots'. In Pittsburgh in June 1946, an estimated crowd of 40,000 queued for a chance to buy just one of the 13,000

A sales assistant showing a pair of nylon stockings in 1946.

pairs of nylons on sale. Nylon became an acceptable material even for haute couture dressmakers. But it couldn't last. The one thing that is certain in life is that women's fashions will change – men's are altogether more lethargic. There was a movement away from artificial fabrics in favour of more natural materials. Nylon and rayon were seen as rather cheap and slightly tawdry. Silk was back, but, of course, in some parts of the world it had never gone away.

When we last looked at the situation in India, there was a healthy industry centred on the great Moghul cities, such as Agra and the magnificent, but now abandoned Fatehpur Sitri. The East India Company had been formed in 1599, with the idea of getting a foothold in the lucrative spice trade. But the Dutch had established a monopoly in the Spice Islands, and so the British turned to India instead, with the hope of finding trade goods that would prove equally profitable. The early years were not a great success. The English merchants attached themselves to the court, but with no great success. Jahangir showed little interest when given the news of a great British naval victory over the Portuguese and was far more impressed by an English mastiff which had successfully fought and killed a leopard. His successor, Shah Jahan, showed an equal lack of interest. But Moghul power was on the wane, and gradually the East India Company's influence grew until it became for a time the de facto ruler of the country. The days of the British Raj had begun. The Company's main objective was not to help local industries prosper, but to make profits to be spent in Britain.

At first, merchants began buying elaborately decorated silk material for the British market, where it proved to be extremely popular – too popular as it turned out. The British weavers objected, and the Company changed tactics. Instead of sending finished cloth, they began sending out yarn instead. It was not a success. Indian raw silk was considered inferior to that from other sources, and the East India Company began losing money. By 1835, the Company had abandoned the silk trade altogether. All this had a devastating effect on the industry as a whole. There was a lack of investment which meant that Indian silk manufacturers were still relying on the handloom for cloth making, and the quality of raw silk declined. Instead of exporting good quality silk, India was mostly sending out waste silk, which fetched a far lower price. The locally reeled silk was described as 'full of knots and loose ends and of unequal strength'. Local weavers preferred to use silk imported from China. G.B. Jathar and S.G. Beri in their book *Indian Economics* published in 1929 quote dramatic figures. The value of silk exported in 1845 was 3,560,000 rupees; in 1925 it was 295,800 rupees.

Jathar and Beri describe the efforts being made in the 1920s to improve the situation. The agricultural department of what was then the Province of Bengal, set up two schools of sericulture. As students graduated, they were given a small grant and 'seed stock' and encouraged to set up rearing houses for the silk moth. As an extra help, the government had also imposed a high tariff on imported silk. There was also at that time a movement to encourage what was in effect a cottage industry to become more efficient. In Bombay, now Mumbai, six weaving schools had already been established. But there was no rush towards industrialisation – quite the opposite. It was deliberate policy to encourage the handloom sector to produce ornate materials specifically aimed at the wealthiest purchaser. The idea of encouraging local handcrafts was also being espoused by a man who was becoming increasingly important in Indian political life, Mahatma Gandhi. He might have been thought to be an enthusiastic encourager of the local silk industry. In fact, he wanted it brought to an end. He was a vegetarian and utterly opposed to the killing of any animals for the benefit of humans. As the silk industry undoubtedly killed the pupae before they had a chance to emerge as moths, the process was inhumane. The argument has appeared again in recent years in the west, raised by animal rights activists with some success. The British fashion company ASOS announced in 2018 that it would no longer be selling any silk products.

Following independence, Indian governments adopted a unique approach to textile production. It was a vital part of the country's economy and clearly needed nurturing. On the other hand, millions depended on it for their livelihood, and a wholesale move to modern factory technology would have resulted in mass unemployment. So, a limit was put on the number of mills that could be built and equipped with new machinery, with an emphasis on co-operative mills. Cloth production was divided between the power loom section, which might involve one man working a single loom or a small workshop, and the handloom section. Travelling around India, one can see this extraordinary diversity; on the one hand, one can visit a factory as modern as any in the world, and then you can go to a village where men are weaving on pit looms. These are just what the name suggests. A pit is dug in the floor and the weaver sits with his feet in the pit, operating the treadles. Most of

Improvisation in modern India; a bicycle wheel being used for silk winding.

these looms have at least been 'modernised' by including the flying shuttle, developed over two centuries ago. Some do not even have that degree of sophistication, but simply pass the shuttle by hand, using a smooth-bottomed 'boat' shuttle. One I brought back as a souvenir sits next to me on the windowsill, and it is indeed very boat-like, with pointed ends and smooth curves. Different regions have their own specialities. In Assam, silk from a local silk moth *Antheraea Assamensis* is used to produce Muga silk, which is notable for its golden lustre. It is so highly prized that once it was only used for royal garments. Today it is a valuable export.

A large part of the industry, however, is simply involved in producing yarn. Statistics for 2018-19 show that sericulture

Extracting muga silk from the cocoons in Assam.

Clothing that displays the magnificent golden texture of muga silk.

was spread across an astonishing 52,360 villages. Altogether, with sericulture and manufacture, the silk industry provides employment for nearly nine million workers. The country is the second most important producer of silk in the world, with annual exports worth over $250 million. The government is pushing for increased production, and one line of approach lies in improving the basic source of the silk – the silk moth itself. The familiar *Bombyx Mori* does not fare well in very hot climates – and Indian summers can be very hot indeed. To combat this, researchers have developed various bivoltine breeds – hybrids that are bred for heat resistance. The Sericulture Research Institute in Andhra Pradesh has recently produced a trans-genic silkworm that not only survives the high temperatures but is also resistant to various viruses that have troubled growers in the past. The new versions are being distributed widely. As in many aspects of Indian life, the silk industry is a mixture of the very traditional and the very modern. Much of the home market is for colourful saris as it has been for centuries, while other materials are being woven to meet the tastes of Western customers, especially in America. The tending of silkworms has scarcely altered, but the worms themselves have been modified by scientists. With such a varied scene, it is difficult to predict where Indian silk might be heading in the future.

Asia has never lost its place as the major centre for silk production, but the industry developed far faster in some parts than in others. Thailand lagged well behind other neighbouring countries; the rich preferred the imported materials from China in particular to anything produced in their own country. That everything changed

Silk weaving in Thailand.

in the twentieth century was mainly down to the efforts of a former American serviceman. Jim Thompson served in the Office of Strategic Services during the Second World War. He travelled widely during the war years and fell in love with Thailand. When he left the OSS in 1946, he made a permanent home in Thailand and, with a partner, set up the Thai Silk Company. He was not interested in modern manufacture but wanted to help revive the rapidly fading handloom industry. He specialised in producing shot silk, a material in which the warp thread is one colour and the weft another. My father worked for many years in Bangkok and I well remember him coming home and bringing Thai silk for my mother. Even as a boy I was impressed by the material, which miraculously, it seemed, constantly changed colour as it was moved about. The material received a huge publicity boost with the appearance of the movie version of *The King and I* in 1956. It won an Academy Award for the gorgeous costumes designed by Irene Sharaff. She used Thai silk, and Americans came to love the material. Paradoxically, the film was banned in Thailand itself because of its portrayal of the king. Jim Thompson was successful in his aim of revitalising the handloom industry as he had hoped, but the story has a curious end. On the wall of his house in Bangkok there is a horoscope predicting that 1967 would be an unlucky year. That year he was in Malaysia, went walking in the forest and was never seen again.

The development of the Asian silk rearing industry brought European developments to a halt. Italy, which had once had a thriving industry, succumbed to cheap Chinese imported yarn and one by one the mills closed until none was left. All that has changed in recent years. The revival owes a great deal to major fashion houses such as Gucci and Valentino, who announced plans to start 1,000 silkworm factories. The process is already under way and is thriving at Como, already well known as a manufacturing centre. There were several reasons for wanting to restart Italian sericulture after a forty years absence, not least economic. The price of Chinese silk has risen sharply to a point where locally produced silk can compete. Labour costs may be far higher in Italy than in China, but transport costs are low and there is no import duty to pay. Sericulture may have changed little, but production techniques have changed enormously. Como has established a reputation for using the latest digital printing technology to produce an exciting new range of designs. And the new designers favour the locally grown silk. None of this will make a huge difference to China, which accounts for over four fifths of world production.

China, however, has its own problem. In recent years, air pollution has risen alarmingly and mulberry trees have been among the victims. And as China develops its industries, the young are showing far less enthusiasm for staying in the country, working on silk farms. They want the city life. In other words, the world of silk is changing, but then it has been changing and developing for over 4,000 years, so there is no reason why it should not do so now and in the future. But one change would never have been anticipated. No one expected a garment to be made from silk that came from any creature apart from the silk moth. But now it has happened.

A silk spinning mill in China in 2018.

CHAPTER THIRTEEN

The Web of Silk

We see natural silk all over the place and probably regard it as a nuisance, sweeping it away with a casual flick. We don't think of it as silk – we call it a cobweb. But the spider is producing a silken thread and doing so in a very sophisticated manner. An article by David Robson in *New Scientist* in February 2020 described how researchers had discovered a surprising intelligence at work in the humble spider. We think of spiders as making silk purely to create a web to catch prey, but they have other more unusual uses as well. Some species use them for 'ballooning'; they send up silken threads to catch the breeze and waft them off to new locations, sensing when the wind is right by hairs on their legs. Even in building their webs, different species use different techniques, and having built them they 'fine tune' them by testing the vibrations in the web and adjusting as necessary. When presented with prey in two locations in a laboratory experiment, the spiders were able in most cases to judge which was the nearer and head straight for it. These and other experiments suggest that, although they have tiny brains, they might have something we recognise as thought processes. So, in many ways, spiders are a lot more interesting than most of us thought. But what interests scientists and others is the nature of the silk.

The fact that is most often quoted about spider silk is that it is stronger than steel, with the suggestion that it is the strongest material known. That is not quite true, Kevlar is stronger. But as well as having great tensile strength, spider silk is also ductile – it can be stretched. This combination of tensile strength and ductility means it can absorb energy without breaking. It is the toughest material we know. With such remarkable properties this is obviously a very valuable material. But spiders are generally rather tiny and produce limited quantities of silk. But could it be used to make textiles?

One man who was convinced there was a future for spider silk was a French naturalist, Bon de Saint Helene, who collected spiders from cottages near his home and used the silk to make a pair of stockings and a pair of gloves in the early 1700s, which he presented to the French Academy. He then became more ambitious and made a garment for Louis XIV to wear but when the king put it on, the whole thing began to disintegrate, to the king's embarrassment and annoyance, and the maker's chagrin. The next attempt to weave with spider silk took place in the nineteenth century. Paul Camboué, a Jesuit missionary and teacher who arrived in Madagascar in 1882, made extensive studies of the local flora and fauna, identifying many species previously unrecorded. One species particularly intrigued him, the golden orb spider. Over 48,000 different species of spider have been identified so far, but this one is remarkable. It is large, about the size of an average hand, but it is the web that is distinctive for the golden colour that gives the creature its name.

Camboué decided to try and use this silk to create textiles. He built a device known as 'the guillotine', simply because the head was held on one side of the wooden contraption and the abdomen was on the other – unlike the lethal device, the spider guillotine left its victim intact and healthy. Once the spider was in place it was only necessary to touch the back of the abdomen with a finger to start the process of producing silk that could then be drawn out. He set up a special spider farm at Tananarive and

The female golden web spider.

employed local girls to reel the silk, spin and weave it. In 1900, he sent a bed canopy to the Paris Exposition, where it was put on display. There was, however, no commercial interest in developing the idea, and no more attempts at weaving from spider silk were made for 100 years.

In 2004, an Englishman, Simon Peers, and an American, Nicholas Godley, decided to resurrect Camboué's idea. They too worked in Madagascar with the female golden orb spider and used a version of the guillotine. Every day, more spiders were collected and brought to the 'spidery' to provide the silk. They were used in batches of 24 to supply 24 strands that could be wound together. In making the garments, threads were doubled to 48 for the lining and doubled again to 96 for the main body of the garments. Many reports quote the fact that a million spiders were used, which is somewhat misleading. In fact, just over 20,000 spiders were brought to the spidery, each of them used several times to create the million threads. Two items were woven on hand looms, a shawl and a cape. The shawl had its pattern woven into the fabric, based on traditional Madagascan motifs. The cape was altogether more elaborate. With complex patterns added by appliqué and embroidery. The finished cape was exhibited at the Victoria and Albert Museum in London in 2012. It is a thing of great beauty and the natural gold colour is quite amazing. But the amount of work that had to go into producing it was immense and took years to complete. It was hardly a system that would seem to have any obvious commercial possibilities, simply because of the costs involved. But it did demonstrate that spider silk had special qualities, both of toughness and beauty that made it desirable. As with the silk of the moth, there was a real incentive to try and produce in the lab what the spider created in the wild.

One of the first to begin tackling this problem was Professor Randy Lewis of Utah State University, who set up a spider silk laboratory. Before you can make artificial silk, you need to know what the natural material consists of. In the 1990s, they cloned spider silk and sequenced the proteins. That was just a start. There were then years of experiments, working out exactly what gave the silk its strength and elasticity. Somewhat surprisingly, the protein found in the silk was also present in goat's milk and experiments were made with modifying the goats genetically to produce fibres. An alternative involved a fermentation process involving genetically modified bacteria. That approach was followed up by a start up

The golden cape made from Madagascan golden orb spider silk, displayed at the Victoria and Albert Museum in 2012.

Company, Bolt Threads, established near San Francisco. They began using the fermentation commercially in a comparatively small way.

A new approach was made at the University of Cambridge. In an article by Emily Matchar in the *Smithsonian Magazine*, July 2017, Darshil Shah of the University's Centre for Natural Material Innovation spelled out the basic problem. 'Spiders are interesting models because they are able to produce these superb silk fibres at room temperature using water as a solvent. This process spiders have evolved over hundreds of millions of years, but we have been unable to copy so far.' The Cambridge team did, however, manage to produce a fibre that started with a mixture that was 98 per cent water. The other two per cent was made up of silica and cellulose, bound together by cucurbiturils – an imposing name, but with a simple origin; these large organic molecules look like Cucurbita – or, in plain English, pumpkins. First synthesised in 1905, these molecules have proved invaluable in holding other large molecules together. The silica and cellulose fibres can be pulled from the gel and within 30 seconds the water has evaporated, leaving strong, stretchy fibres behind. They are not quite as strong as natural spider silk but come very close. This system has huge advantages in that it works at room temperature with materials which are readily available and no chemical solvents are required. It is a remarkably green process, and if it can be scaled up offers all kinds of possibilities, including using different basic raw materials to create new fibres. The problem Shah and the team face is scaling up a process from laboratory to production. But with so many groups now working on developing artificial spider silk, there seems little doubt they will succeed. This is still early days; after all it took two decades of research and development to get nylon manufactured.

Silk has come a long way since the time thousands of years ago when, according to the legend, a cocoon fell into a princess's tea. Its appeal has never waned. Its lustrous nature, its softness, durability and its adaptability have made silk fabrics the most desirable of all textiles, not just in the land where the humble moth first gave up its secrets, but around the globe. And, in travelling, silk has taken with it knowledge and ideas, inventions and discoveries. Silk seems to turn up everywhere, from the first tentative attempts at flight to the development of the computer. The book you are reading was made possible because the technology of paper making came to the west down the Silk Road. That useful little number that tells you which page you were on is the result of an Indian system of numerals that travelled the same route and the words you are reading were produced on a system that developed from an idea first devised to automate the weaving of complex patterns in silk. There is also a continuity; techniques passed down through the generations sit beside the latest technology. This was brought home to me at the heart of the European industry in Lyon. In the morning, I visited a craftsman working at a handloom, producing ornate fabrics, while in the afternoon I went just a short distance to a modern factory where the shuttleless looms were turning out equally ornate fabrics

Modern technology can produce beautiful and elaborate clothes to match those of the past; a diaphanous silk dress produced on an electrically powered loom.

at an astonishing rate, guided only by a computer programme. Over the years, scientists have attempted to produce a material that has all the qualities of silk; they have come close but have yet to reach their goal. Silk has been called the 'Queen of fabrics'; the queen it seems will reign for many years to come.

Select Bibliography

BAKER, Patricia L., *Islamic Textiles,* British Museum Press, 1995

BRACKETT, L. P., *The Silk Industry in America,* 1862

ENGLISH, W., *The Textile Industry,* 1969

HANSEN, Valerie, *The Silk Road,* OUP USA, 2012

JATHERS, G.B. and BERI, S.G., *Indian Economics,* 1931

POLO, Marco, LATHAM, r (translator and editor) , *The Travels,* Penguin Classics, 2015

MILLS, L.J. (ed), *The Textile Educator (3 vols),* 1927

SINGER, Charles, HOLMROYD, E.J., HALL, A.R., WILLIAMS, Trevor I. (eds), *A History of Technology (7 volumes),* 1954-78

STEIN, Aurel, *Ruins of Desert Cathay,* 1912

VAINKER, Shelagh, *Chinese Silk; A Cultural History,* British Museum Press, 2004

WARNER, Sir Frank, *The Silk Industry of the United Kingdom,* Forgotten Books, 2004

Index